Home Office Research Study 213

An exploration of decision-making at discretionary lifer panels

Nicola Padfield and Alison Liebling
with Helen Arnold
Institute of Criminology
University of Cambridge 2000

Home Office Research, Development and Statistics Directorate
December 2000

Home Office Research Studies

The Home Office Research Studies are reports on research undertaken by or on behalf of the Home Office. They cover the range of subjects for which the Home Secretary has responsibility. Titles in the series are listed at the back of this report (copies are available from the address on the back cover). Other publications produced by the Research, Development and Statistics Directorate include Research Findings, the Research Bulletin, Statistical Bulletins and Statistical Papers.

The Research, Development and Statistics Directorate

RDS is part of the Home Office. The Home Office's purpose is to build a safe, just and tolerant society in which the rights and responsibilities of individuals, families and communities are properly balanced and the protection and security of the public are maintained.

RDS is also a part of the Government Statistical Service (GSS). One of the GSS aims is to inform Parliament and the citizen about the state of the nation and provide a window on the work and performance of government, allowing the impact of government policies and actions to be assessed.

Therefore -

Research Development and Statistics Directorate exists to improve policy making, decision taking and practice in support of the Home Office purpose and aims, to provide the public and Parliament with information necessary for informed debate and to publish information for future use.

"The views expressed in this report are those of the authors, not necessarily those of the Home Office (nor do they reflect Government policy)."

First published 2000
Application for reproduction should be made to the Communications and Development Unit, Room 201, Home Office, 50 Queen Anne's Gate, London SW1H 9AT.
© Crown copyright 2000   ISBN   1 84082 568 5
                          ISSN   0072 6435

Discretionary Lifer Panels (DLPs) were introduced in 1992 following a decision of the European Court of Human Rights. This established the right of those serving discretionary life sentences to regular and independent review after the tariff (punishment) part of their sentence had been served.

This first study of DLPs examines the process in depth. It looks at the style and actions of the panels, the views of the participants and the extent to which quality and effectiveness was evident in decision-making. It brings together empirical research and legal argument well and should be of interest both to those directly involved with DLPs and to those interested in the balance between public protection and human rights.

Chris Lewis
Head of Offenders and Corrections Unit
Research Development and Statistics Directorate

Acknowledgements

We would like to thank Joy Anderson, Maureen Colledge, Tom Ellis, Loraine Gelsthorpe, Adrian Grounds, Katie Holloway, Roger Hood, Marie Howes, Terry McCarthy, Colleen Moore, Tim Morris, Jeremy Page, Stephen Shute, Nigel Walker, Mollie Weatheritt, Leanne Weber, Pam Wilson, and the Lifer Governors, Lifer Liaison Officers, Parole Board members, prisoners and prison staff who have been so helpful to us.

We would also like to express our appreciation to Professor Anthony Bottoms for so enthusiastically engaging with us as we clarified our ideas, and for devoting so much of his time to our research. He is a co-author of our concluding chapter (Chapter 6).

After a little initial hesitation at the prospect of being so closely watched, the vast majority of our panel members became open and accommodating. We are grateful to them for their hospitality and generosity in answering our questions.

This was a short exploratory and observational project looking at the operation of panel hearings over a nine month period. Our contract specified that Alison Liebling and Nicola Padfield would spend a minimum of 20 days each on the project. In the end, we spent more like 100 days each on the project. We had a full-time research assistant (Helen Arnold) and a part-time research administrator (Joy Anderson, followed by Colleen Moore). This project was in every sense a team enterprise and we would like to record our thanks to Helen and Colleen for working so hard and so efficiently with us.

Nicola Padfield
Alison Liebling

"I think it's important, right, that every lifer be given the opportunity to speak to the people that make decisions on their life, you know. A bit of paper is flat and emotionless and expressionless. It's open to interpretation and anyone can read what's said, but when I'm here and I'm talking and I'm responding to what you're saying and if you have any doubt, you can question me on that doubt, that is the benefit. It also...made me feel a lot better about me, that at least I've gone in there and I've put my point of view across and whatever, at least I've had the opportunity to do that. And these people now have something more to contend with than a dead bit of paper, you know. It was satisfying in that respect." (Prisoner)

"In making judgements about release or restraint, a parole board is engaged in the appearance of condoning or condemning criminal behaviour; it is making statements about good and evil, desert and punishment, to the prisoner, the institution, and the wider community. The parole decision, in short, is symbolically significant." (Hawkins, 1983: 102)

"It's all about people, isn't it? It's all about the quality of the psychiatrist and the judge and the independent member." (Judge).

Contents

Abbreviations

AMPLG	Adult Males, Parole and Lifer Group
DLP	Discretionary Lifer Panel
DLS	Discretionary Life Sentence
ECHR	European Court of Human Rights/European Convention on Human Rights
EHRR	European Human Rights Reports
ETS	Enhanced Thinking Skills (an accredited offending behaviour course)
HEO	Higher Executive Officer (civil service grade)
HMP	Her Majesty's Pleasure
LLO	Lifer Liaison Officer
LSIR	Level of Service Inventory Revised
LMU	Lifer Management Unit
LRU	Lifer Review Unit
MDT	Mandatory Drug Testing
MLP	Mandatory Lifer Panel
NUD*IST	Non-numerical Unstructured Data Indexing, Searching and Theory-building
PPG	Penile Plethysmograph
PRES	Pre-Release Employment Scheme
R&R	Reasoning and Rehabilitation (an accredited offending behaviour course)
SOTP	Sex Offender Treatment Programme

Executive summary

Introduction

This research constituted an observational study of the nature and quality of decision-making at Discretionary Lifer Panels. DLPs were introduced in 1992 following a decision of the European Court of Human Rights establishing the right of those subject to discretionary life sentences to regular and independent review once the tariff (punishment) part of their sentence had ended. Discretionary life sentences are imposed where an offence is considered grave enough to require a very long sentence, the offender is a person of mental instability who poses a grave danger to the public, and it appears that the offender will remain unstable and a potential danger for a long or uncertain time. Continuing detention, once the 'relevant' (tariff) part of the sentence has been served, can only be justified on the grounds that an individual's release poses an unacceptable risk to the public.

This decision-making task was given to the Parole Board, who sit in panels of three, chaired by a judge. Panels can direct release or recommend a move to open conditions. The decision is taken at an oral hearing at which the prisoner can be legally represented. The hearing should avoid formality in the proceedings, but should follow a broadly court-like process, with the evidence fully considered and questions to witnesses permissible. Clear and cogent reasons should be given to the prisoner. The level of risk presented should be 'a substantial risk of further offences dangerous to life or limb'. The Parole Board has to carry out a balancing exercise 'between the legitimate conflicting interests of both prisoner and public'. Since 1992, about 200 DLP cases have been considered each year. Seventeen per cent of those resulted in a direction for release, although this figure has declined from 20 per cent in 1993 to nine per cent in 1998–9. A further 20 per cent per year have been recommended for transfer to open conditions. Eleven released discretionary life sentence prisoners were recalled to prison in 1998–9, compared with 4 in 1993.

Aims

The aims of the research were to establish how DLPs operate; whether the process is fair; the effectiveness and consistency of the process; the effectiveness of panel members in performing their role; how panels assess risk; the level of user-friendliness of panels; and the extent to which they represent value for money.

Methods

The research was carried out between March and December 1999. After a period of pilot work, information was collected on a total of 69 cases. Fifty-two cases were observed (49 including the deliberations, normally held in private). These hearings took place in 22 different establishments. Eight of the observed cases were recalled prisoners. An analytic guide was developed and used throughout the observations. These were supplemented with 40 formal, tape-recorded semi-structured interviews carried out with participants in the process and 15 semi-formal discussions with others. The observation and interview data were systematically coded and analysed using a qualitative computer-aided programme.

Main findings

The key decision whether to direct for release or recommend for transfer to open conditions rested on a prior decision taken, often rather implicitly, about risk. The moment of decision-making began well before the formal hearing, but the oral hearing could influence panels in either direction. The question of risk assessment was approached fairly consistently. It was an extremely difficult task. A cumulative picture was formed of the prisoner from the dossier and throughout the hearing. Panels arrived at hearings with concerns they wished to address. They looked for evidence of change, insight into the offence, evidence of offending behaviour work successfully undertaken and realistic release plans, with the prospect of effective supervision. They also took account of behaviour in prison, security classification, relationships with family, the nature of the index offence, attitude towards the victim and other risk factors such as medical treatment. There was a certain 'intuition gradient' in the decision-making process. Sometimes personal characteristics or cultural factors seemed to influence decisions. There was scope for bias to be checked during the deliberations because of the composition of the panel. Level of risk was rarely discussed and the Board operated with extreme caution.

Panel members spent considerable amounts of time reading the dossiers and preparing for hearings. The judge as Chairman received the dossier before the other panel members and the directions he or she gave at this stage were important in avoiding deferrals. The hearing could be divided into four stages: the pre-hearing discussion; the hearing; the deliberation; and the drafting of the reasons for the decision. At the pre-hearing discussion, panel members explored the key issues and exchanged provisional views on the likely outcome. At the hearing the evidence was tested through the questioning of witnesses. The composition of the panel often facilitated a very careful consideration of the case. The nature of the hearing varied according to whether panels were being asked to direct release or transfer to open conditions. However panels, as a process, were conducted remarkably consistently. Too much formality or informality could handicap the process. The level of informality largely depended on the personal style of the judge as Chair. Panels made swift decisions at the deliberation stage. There was often considerable consensus. Panels spent considerable time drafting the reasons for the decision and while doing this continued to comment on the strength of the evidence and the factors which influenced their decision. Panels were constrained by their formal terms of reference; yet they often recommended other progressive moves. They often used the decision letter to fulfil many functions including relaying a message to the Prison Service.

A number of separate themes emerged from our observations which merited separate consideration. Late papers were often received on the morning of the hearing or shortly before the panel met. Dossiers were comprehensive and carefully presented. Despite a certain amount of repetition they were of a high standard. Delays to the process were frequent. Nineteen per cent of the cases in our original sample were deferred before the hearing, mostly for reasons beyond the panel's control. The DLP process successfully moved some prisoners through the lifer system, but it also inadvertently slowed some prisoners' progress down (for example, the provisional timetable for hearings was fixed some eight or nine months in advance, and a prisoner might not be moved on to another prison if he/she was 'waiting' for a hearing). There were some differences between first oral recall hearings and ordinary DLPs. The focus of the evidence was on 'what went wrong' in the community rather than on any release plan. Panels were confirming the recall decision and considering whether it was still necessary for the protection of the public that the prisoner should be confined.

The role played by each panel member varied: judges chaired proceedings with varying degrees of formality; psychiatrists often played a key role, particularly in cases where mental disorders were present. A few psychiatrists withdrew from the panel discussion when psychiatric issues were not pertinent. Independent members acted as the voice of 'joe public' and of other criminal justice agencies. The composition of the panel was effective. The three panel members together provided a balance, requiring different professional and lay perspectives to be reconciled. Whilst panel secretaries were successful in achieving the logistical demands of their role, they varied in their level of involvement and in the nature of the advice they gave. Witnesses played a very influential role, although their appearance at hearings seemed haphazard. The prisoner's role was pivotal, and was assisted by good, realistic legal representation. Prisoners found the experience difficult and many were very nervous but they perceived the oral hearing as a reasonably fair and open process compared with decisions taken on paper. Panels approached specialist reports in a discriminating and robust way, and were also prepared to 'test' home probation officers, psychiatrists and psychologists in a probing way. The Secretary of State's view was frequently supplied late, and was often routinised and sometimes out-of-date. However, it had two important functions: it was referred to by the panel as they finalised the written decision; and when it was received on time it was useful to legal representatives as they prepared the legal case for the prisoner. The impact of the Secretary of State's representative was very variable and frequently minor.

We found it difficult to draw conclusions about the quality and effectiveness of the process without considering the aims of the DLP and the appropriate terms of reference. There was a tension between the need to be cautious and the need to be fair. The current position, where positive recommendations outside the formal terms of reference were frequently made, was confusing, but seemed to achieve a compromise most people could live with. There was considerable support for extending the terms of reference to make panel recommendations on early review binding.

Conclusions and implications

In our analysis of the data, we considered seven key conceptual issues:

(i) *The significance of a prisoner being 'post-tariff'*. There is a paradox in that DLPs were created in response to the ECHR recognition of the special status of 'post-tariff' lifers, yet such special status plays almost no part in the thinking of DLPs due to their concentration on issues of current risk.

(ii) *Giving proper recognition to competing rights.* A framework of 'competing rights' helps to provide an analytic framework encompassing both substantive and procedural fairness, and can guide the way risk is assessed.

(iii) *The Parole Board as court.* The Parole Board should act as a 'court'. Recommendations made by the Parole Board should give the prisoner a public law 'legitimate expectation'. Unless the Prison Service rejects a recommendation within a certain time and with written reasons, it should become binding.

(iv) *The relationship between the Parole Board (DLP) and the Prison and Probation Services.* Concerns were raised by evidence that prisoners 'got stuck in the system', or when it seemed that a prisoner stayed in prison simply because courses from which he/she would benefit were available in prison but not in the community. Closer working between the Prison Service and the Probation Service may reduce this problem.

(v) *Burdens of proof.* Panels sometimes appeared to feel that the prisoner had a 'persuasive' burden of proof. Yet some lawyers suggested that the Home Secretary should have the burden of proving that the prisoner is not safe to be released. Discussion of a 'burden of proof' was misleading: instead the DLP should operate with two legal presumptions:

- a safety presumption: they cannot release unless they are satisfied that 'it is no longer necessary for the protection of the public that the prisoner should be confined'

- a human rights presumption: post-tariff discretionary lifers must be released as soon as possible, and should be given every opportunity to be 'tested for safety'.

(vi) *An inquisitorial or an adversarial process?* The process should be largely inquisitorial so that Panels can be consciously proactive in two senses:

- testing for risk/safety

- testing whether the Prison and Probation Services are respecting the prisoners' human rights.

(vii) *The status of 'risk factors' as indicators of risk.* The extent to which the risk factors considered really are indicators of risk is not explored: it may be that some of the beliefs on which the decision-making process is based are unfounded. Some validated risk factors were not discussed during the decision-making process; others were considered haphazardly. The research questions whether what panels did during a hearing could accurately be called 'risk assessment', without more standardised and validated techniques at their disposal.

Conclusions

Any exclusive emphasis on the operation of the discretionary lifer panel process may cloud the larger question of the fairness of the substantive outcome. Whilst the Parole Board may direct release, no prisoner whose case was observed during this study was released unless he/she was in open conditions. When the Parole Board recommended a transfer to open conditions, the Secretary of State held the trump card and could veto (or delay) the transfer.

For prisoners, and indeed for all those involved, the DLP process was hugely significant. Yet it appeared that the key decisions were taken at the transfer stage and that the power to make these decisions rested firmly with the Prison Service and the Home Secretary. The power of the Parole Board to direct release was seriously constrained by powers and inertias lying elsewhere.

If a narrow view of the process is taken, then the DLP process is fair. The quality of the decision-making process was high and decisions were reached carefully and after thorough consideration of all the available information. Yet when seen in its fuller context, it seemed less fair. The significance of a prisoner being post-tariff and the dual task of the DLP needed emphasising.

The question of effectiveness depends on the criteria used. On the terms of reference currently applied, decision-making seemed effective. Yet, judging the DLP as a 'court', it clearly has limited powers and limited effect. If the role of the DLP as 'court' was strengthened, perhaps the significant problems of late reports and delayed hearings would decrease.

Procedurally we concluded that DLPs acted consistently. Inconsistencies of style were observed, but these inconsistencies had little effect on the consistency of the decision-making process. In any case, consistency was rightly regarded as a qualified good. Panels generally made strenuous efforts to be user friendly. Too much of a departure from formality could be disarming and frustrating for the other participants. Individual panel members brought their professional expertise to the task: their effectiveness in performing this role was diminished when the procedure became too 'adversarial' rather than 'inquisitorial'.

One of the panel's key tasks is the assessment of risk: an extremely difficult task, particularly with this group of prisoners. The style of risk assessment was more clinical than actuarial, and seemed cautious. Panels need to weigh both seriousness and certainty of risk, yet seemed to avoid discussing *levels* of risk.

The recall process raises particular concerns. Whilst recall hearings were conducted similarly to ordinary DLPs, the issues raised were very different. In a recall case, the panel was being asked not only to assess risk, but to confirm the recall of someone who had previously been deemed safe to release if managed adequately in the community. The reality of power in recall cases seemed to lie with the Probation Service. The human rights implications of this are too easily ignored. The management of risk needs carefully distinguishing from the assessment of risk.

Do panel hearings represent value for money? Given the human rights obligations of the Parole Board, the relative expense of the process is justified. Resources are wasted in delays and deferrals, but if the positive duty on the Prison Service to move post-tariff prisoners swiftly towards release were acted on, this would save money.

Whilst Parliament seems to have tipped the scales in favour of protecting the public, the competing rights of the prisoner need all the more protection.

Recommendations

- The significance of a prisoner being 'post-tariff' needs to be underlined.

- The DLP should be recognised as 'court-like' and perhaps renamed as a Parole Court for this purpose.

- Recommendations made by the Parole Board should, unless rejected by the Home Secretary within a fixed time-frame and with written reasons, create 'legitimate expectations' for prisoners which could be subject to judicial review.

- Since the DLP is a court, documents not produced in advance should not be admitted at the hearing.

- Panels should separate the decision about risk (and the reasons for that) from the decision about directions or recommendations (and the reasons for that). This two-stage process would lead to more explicit decision-making, and greater consistency of approach.

- In recall cases, panels should separate the confirmation of the recall decision from the current risk assessment.

- There is a need for more training and procedural guidance. In particular, the empirical status of risk factors should be available to all participants in the process; panel secretaries and Secretary of State's representatives require guidance on role.

- There should be more formal feedback from the Prison Service on the outcome of recommendations and to the Prison Service on the quality and timeliness of reports.

- Further research on the effective management of life sentence prisoners (including their movement through categories) should be carried out.

Part one   Introduction

"....[T]he best way to protect you from committing such an attack and to ensure that you will not be at liberty until the risk of such an attack has gone – is to pass a sentence of life imprisonment, not, of course...with the intent that you should stay in prison for the rest of your life, but with the intent that you should not be released until those responsible for the supervision of your case are satisfied that it is safe" (Sentencing Judge)

1   Introduction and methods

Introduction

In December 1998 we were invited to reply to a competitive tender for a small piece of research on the operation of Discretionary Lifer Panels under the heading Improving Decision-Making: Life Sentenced Prisoners. Nicola Padfield, an academic lawyer and qualified barrister, and Alison Liebling, an experienced prisons researcher, decided to pool their different academic resources in order to place a bid for what seemed to constitute an exciting opportunity to learn more about an important area of criminal justice practice and decision-making[1]. The bid was successful and this report is an account of the research and its findings.

Discretionary Lifer Panels were created after the decision of the European Court of Human Rights in *Thynne, Wilson and Gunnell* [13 EHRR 666]. This case established that those subject to a discretionary life sentence should be entitled to a regular review of the legality of their detention in a court, independent of the executive. The Parole Board carry out this responsibility, in panels consisting of three members. Discretionary Lifer Panels have now been in place for seven years. At the time this research began, a total of 1,271 cases had been considered. The Parole Board had directed release in 17 per cent of cases, and recommended transfer to open conditions in 20 per cent of cases. In 1998–9, 291 cases were considered at an average cost of £1,286 per case. Twenty-six prisoners had been recommended for release (9%) and 43 were recommended for transfer to open conditions (Home Office, 1999a). The trend has been to release a diminishing proportion of prisoners whose cases have been considered[2].

This research is an exploration of the nature and quality of this decision-making process. It constitutes primarily an observational study. It examines all stages of the current DLP procedures, in particular the conduct of panels and how decisions are made about risk assessment, the granting or refusing of release, or recommending a move to open prison.

---

1. There were at that time, three other research projects on aspects of decision-making being carried out by colleagues at the Institute of Criminology which strengthened our interest and motivation to do the research: a study of mental health tribunals (Holloway, 2000), a study of immigration detention decisions (Weber and Gelsthorpe, 2000), and a study of decisions to detain in psychiatric hospitals (Gelsthorpe, Howes and Grounds, 2000). This research has benefited from the support and shared interest of the above projects.
2. The average figure masks a declining percentage of cases where release is directed, from 27 per cent in 1994 to 9 per cent in 1998–9. This declining percentage may, of course, reflect many factors such as the nature of the cases or the recommendations of report writers, as well as increasing caution on the part of the Parole Board.

Our original proposal suggested that we might concentrate on three different aspects of the process: the quality of the dossiers; the DLP hearing itself and the human rights implications of the decision-making process. As a result of discussions with the Home Office and the Parole Board, we were invited to concentrate rather less on the dossiers or the human rights implications and much more on what happened during the hearings[3]. The overall aims of the research then, were to establish:

- whether the DLP process is fair
- the effectiveness and consistency of the DLP process
- the extent to which the conduct of hearings varies between release and recall cases
- the effectiveness of panels in performing their role
- how panels assess risk (including assessing what information has most impact)
- the level of user-friendliness of panels
- the extent to which panel hearings represent value for money.

Although the research was to be mainly observational, it was supported by a number of formal interviews and consultation of dossiers. As the project was exploratory, we built in a pilot stage. This enabled us to familiarise ourselves with the DLP process, raise issues informally with panel members and other participants, develop relevant questions and discuss the research with each other and with interested others.

The research was carried out between March and December 1999. During the pilot stage (March–May 1999), we observed three panels, who conducted a total of six hearings. We attended these hearings together, discussing all aspects of our observations and research methods fully with each other. We designed our observation checklist and our interview schedules throughout this stage, checking our key questions against the terms of reference and against the views of our research steering group[4]. For each hearing attended, we received dossiers in advance and were able to read them in full. We also received a copy of the letter subsequently sent to the prisoner.

For the main study, information was collected on a total of 69 cases (i.e. different dossiers) for which we were provided with the paperwork and intended to observe the oral hearing. However, of the 69 cases, 13 (19%) were deferred before the date of the hearing and were not reconsidered during the research period and three (4%) were not observed due to the

---

3. Most of our research sponsors felt that the dossiers were in general very good and not in need of too much critical analysis; we will return to this point later in our report. The Prison Service also felt that they would learn more than enough about the human rights implications from judicial reviews and other Human Rights Act litigation, so that this task could safely be left to practising lawyers.
4. These are included in Appendix 3.

prisoner objecting to a research presence. One case was observed but adjourned on the date of the hearing and was later observed when the same panel reconvened and is therefore counted as one hearing. Therefore in total 52 different cases were observed during the course of the research. However, in three of the 52 cases the deliberations were not observed, at the request of the panel Chairman. Of the 52 cases, five (9.5%) were observed but were deferred at the hearing and two (4%) became paper hearings as the prisoners did not wish to attend the hearing. We observed a total of 30 different panels and 15 different judges chairing the panels. We observed DLPs in 22 different prison establishments. A breakdown of the hearings observed is shown in Table 1.1.

Table 1.1: *Analysis of hearings*

	Number of cases	
Information collected	69	
Deferred before the hearing date	13	(19%)
Not observed due to prisoner's objection	3	(4%)
Hearings observed	52*	
Deliberations not observed	3	(6%)
Observed but deferred at the hearing	5	(9.5%)
Paper hearings	2	(4%)
Hearings observed (including deliberations) and completed	42	
Number of different judges observed	*15*	
Number of different panels observed	*30*	

* The case which was observed twice is counted as one hearing (see text).

Figure 1.1: *Observations (based on 52 hearings)*

Observations by prison establishment

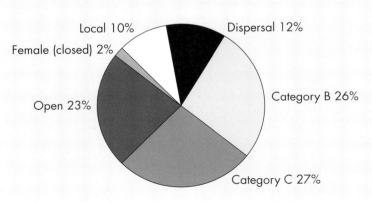

Local 10%
Dispersal 12%
Female (closed) 2%
Category B 26%
Open 23%
Category C 27%

In terms of prisoners' status, of the 52 cases, eight (15%) were recalled prisoners (four of whom had been sentenced to be detained at Her Majesty's Pleasure[5]); 11 (21%) had been sentenced at Her Majesty's Pleasure and 33 (63%) were 'ordinary' discretionary lifer cases. Of the recall cases observed, five hearings were the first DLP since recall and three were subsequent hearings.

Of the 13 cases that were deferred before the date for which the hearing was listed, four were deferred in order that the prisoner could complete an offending behaviour programme, four as a result of late reports, two were due to imminent transfers, one because the tariff had not expired, one not known, and one for further assessment.

Of the five cases that we observed which were deferred, each was for a different reason: because a witness did not attend, to allow time for assessment, due to late reports, pending the outcome of adjudication, and because the prisoner wished for legal representation.

We carried out formal follow-up interviews with a total of 40 participants[6]. These semi-structured interviews were tape-recorded and transcribed in full. We also held semi-formal discussions during which notes were taken with at least 15 participants.

In many cases, two members of the team observed each hearing. This was useful as we each took notes, and we could discuss our observations afterwards. As in any research, this served as a useful check on the validity of our impressions, and enabled a certain amount of division of labour when it came to follow up interviews and informal discussions. These were often held over lunch, at the end of the day, or at a separately arranged time and venue (several in people's homes). Our notes on the observations included a full record of proceedings, some verbatim remarks, and – to a limited extent – our own commentary on what we saw. We used an observation schedule, completed in part during the hearing and in more detail afterwards, to ensure systematic recording of relevant issues. Notes were typed up after each hearing, and our own commentary could be expanded upon as details were remembered.

We developed a case database recording details on each of the panels we expected to attend. These included details of the prisoner, his or her index offence, current location, tariff, previous hearings held, and so on. This was used to place the cases we observed in the context of the total numbers arranged and to make available descriptive information on basic features of the cases we observed.

---

5.   Were under the age of 18 when they committed an offence of murder. Although HMPs are 'mandatory' lifers, they are included in the DLP process (see s 28(1)(b) Crime (Sentences) Act 1997 and Appendix 1). Details of the index offence and time served by prisoners in our sample are to be found in Appendix 2.
6.   Formal interviews were carried out with five judges, four psychiatrists, four independent members, two panel secretaries, seven prisoners, four legal representatives, five lifer governors/liaison officers, two probation officers, two psychologists and five others involved in the process. Semi-formal discussions were carried out with others.

Key research questions

Our key research questions, which we will address fully in Part Two of this report, were refined throughout the project[7] and in the end were as follows:

- How do DLPs operate?
- How consistent is the process?
- What are the key differences between different hearings (if any)?
- Are any differences in process defensible?
- Are there differences between recall cases and ordinary DLPs?
- How formal or informal is the process?
- What are the advantages and disadvantages of any informality?
- How effective are panels in their decision-making?
- What is the quality of decision-making?
- What do panels make decisions about?
- How do panels evaluate risk?
- How effective are they in hearing and testing the evidence?
- How important is experience among legal representatives? Do they understand what DLPs are for?
- What do participants think of the experience (especially perceptions of fairness)?
- What are the implications of the tariff?
- What are the views on the accuracy, quality and timeliness of reports?
- What are the views on the timetable?
- Are the reasons given in decision letters clear, cogent, and helpful?
- What problems arise when the evidence is in dispute?
- Who controls proceedings?
- Is the pre-hearing review adequate?
- Could the process be more efficient without reducing quality?

Data analysis

As this was intended to be a largely qualitative and exploratory study, we have included all of the material in our analysis. Transcribed interviews, typed up fieldwork (observation) notes and other materials (such as the text of the Secretary of State's view and the Panel's

---

7. Our key research questions were refined throughout the project, but the precise terms such as 'effective', 'fairness', 'formal and informal' became increasingly difficult to define. We return to these questions in Chapter Six.

decision letter) were systematically coded and thematically analysed with the aid of a computer-assisted non-numeric data sorting programme (NUD*IST)[8]. This enabled themes identified during the research process to be used to structure the data and ensure comprehensive and accurate reporting. We held regular team meetings, during which we discussed our own observations and emerging thoughts, refined and attempted to address our key questions and come to a consensus about the main issues. Analytic themes were generated via these discussions, consultation of the literature and from reading and re-reading our own notes. Like the panels we had observed, the discussions held served as an invaluable tool for checking different perspectives and forming a judgement.

Scope and approach of the study

This was a short study and one that was largely limited to the observation of one stage in a long and multi-stage process. Whilst we were able to take some account of the preparation and other important stages of the process, this project mainly explores the mechanics of the hearing and the deliberative process. We are aware of other comparable decision-making processes (for example, Mandatory Lifer Panels and Mental Health Review Tribunals) but this study precluded any systematic comparative work. We are aware of some of the useful existing literature on parole decision-making and we have sought, where time has allowed, to take this into account in our analysis (e.g. Hood and Shute, 1999; Cullen and Newell,1999; Coker and Martin, 1985).

Our focus then, is mainly on the hearing as it takes place 'on the day'. We were invited to look mainly at the decision-making process in detail, rather than on outcomes or on large quantifiable aspects of the process. Key changes to some aspects of the procedure were being introduced at the time of the study (for example, the issuing of a new Lifer Manual, the introduction of an audit process for the timely completion of reports, the development of guidance on the process). A user-group had been established to contribute to improvement of the process. As in most social research, we were observing a moving target.

We intended at the outset to follow a broadly qualitative approach because of the exploratory, inductive nature of our research task. This approach is suited to a complex, underexplored setting, where multiple realities are likely to be found. Themes emerge largely from the process of the study, rather than being identified in advance[9]. We were not testing hypotheses, but generating understanding. In this sense, our study is more descriptive than explanatory, but we shall endeavour to account for what we observed.

8. Non-Numerical Unstructured Data Indexing, Searching and Theory-building.
9. We describe our role as researchers, and the research experience in Appendix 4.

The significance of the study

We hope that this research is of considerable interest for three main reasons. First, the underexplored nature of decision-making, both in the parole process but also in general, constitutes a significant gap in criminal justice research. Secondly, we hope that this research will generate useful material, which might assist in training and development. Thirdly, we hope that it will contribute to broader debates about the nature and legitimacy of the life sentence, the operation of parole, the nature of risk assessment and the procedures of decision-making in criminal justice arenas.

In the remainder of this part of our report, we undertake some important preliminary tasks: we outline the current procedures relating to discretionary life sentence prisoners, and offer some descriptive information pertaining to the current discretionary lifer population. In Part Two we report on our research findings in full, and in Part Three we consider the implications of our research and issues arising from it.

2   The discretionary life sentence and release provisions

Introduction

This chapter sets out to explain the legal developments that led to the creation of DLPs in 1992. It explains the different sorts of life sentences that may be imposed, and the role of both the sentencing judge and the Parole Board in the discretionary life sentence process. The DLP is now governed by the Parole Rules 1997. The panel is empowered to direct release or to recommend transfer to open conditions from closed, and a prisoner is entitled to a DLP hearing every two years. Since the only legal remedy from a decision of the DLP is judicial review, the role of the High Court is also reviewed. The chapter ends with a description of the wider context of the life sentence process.

Life sentences

A life sentence is mandatory where a person is convicted of murder, and automatic on those sentenced for a second serious sexual or violent offence which could carry a life sentence (see s2 of the Crime (Sentences) Act 1997). Those under the age of 18 who have been convicted of murder are detained at Her Majesty's Pleasure, and although this is mandatory, they are treated in practice as discretionary life sentence prisoners. A life sentence is a possible (i.e. discretionary) sentence for a number of offences such as: attempted murder; manslaughter; rape; robbery; arson; criminal damage with intent to endanger life; aggravated burglary; kidnapping; incest; sexual intercourse with a girl under the age of 13; infanticide; possessing a Class A drug for supply; unlawful abortion; and forgery of births, deaths or marriage certificates.

The use of discretionary life sentences appears to have developed during the 1950s, as a judicial response to concern over dangerous offenders. As Table 2.1 shows, the number of mandatory and discretionary life sentence prisoners is growing rapidly.

Table 2.1:   *Life sentence and discretionary life sentence prisoners 1970–1999[10]*

Year	Lifer population in prison	Mandatory life prisoners	Discretionary life prisoners
1970	566	415	151
1980	1,584	1,178	406
1990	2,795	2,237	558
1998	3,934	3,114	820
1999	4,206	3,173	1,033

The criteria to be met before a court should impose a discretionary life sentence were set out by the Court of Appeal in *Hodgson* (1967) 52 Cr App R 113:

i.   the offence must in itself be grave enough to require a very long sentence

ii.   the offender must be a person of mental instability who, if at liberty, will probably reoffend and present a grave danger to the public

iii.   it must appear that the offender will remain unstable and a potential danger for a long or uncertain time.

Lord Lane CJ in *Wilkinson* (1983) 5 Cr App R (S) 105 said that,

"it seems to us that a sentence of life imprisonment, other than for an offence when the sentence is obligatory, is really appropriate and must only be passed in the most exceptional circumstances. With a few exceptions .... it is reserved, broadly speaking, for offenders who for one reason or another cannot be dealt with under the Mental Health Act, yet who are in a mental state which makes them dangerous to the life or limb of members of the public. It is sometimes impossible to say when that danger will subside, and therefore an indeterminate sentence is required, so that the prisoner's progress may be monitored by those who have him under their supervision."

More recently, the Court of Appeal in *Attorney-General's Reference (No 32 of 1996) (R v Whittaker)* [1997] 1 Cr App R (S) 261 held that there were two pre-conditions for the imposition of a discretionary life sentence:

i.   the offence must be very serious

10. Source: Home Office, 2000, and earlier years, Prison Statistics, England and Wales for figures from 1980. 1970 figures from Home Office computer records.

ii.   there should be good grounds for believing that the offender might remain a serious danger to the public for a period which could not be reliably estimated at the date of sentence. The grounds which would found such a belief would often relate to the mental condition of the offender, but the crucial question was his or her dangerousness.

In June 1999, there were 1,033 prisoners serving discretionary life sentences in England and Wales (25% of the total lifer population of 4,206 prisoners). The discretionary lifer population can be analysed as shown in Table 2.2.

Table 2.2: *Discretionary lifer population, June 1999*[11]

	Male	Female	TOTAL
Manslaughter/other offence of violence	487	14	501
Sexual offences	382	0	382
Arson	90	10	100
Other	49	1	50
TOTAL	1,008	25	1,033

The legal role of the Parole Board

The law relating to discretionary life sentences was fundamentally changed as a result of the European Court of Human Rights decision in *Thynne, Wilson and Gunnell* (13 EHRR 666). This decision established that once a discretionary life sentence prisoner had served the 'tariff' period set by reference to the index offence, he or she was entitled to have the lawfulness of his or her detention reviewed by a court or tribunal which is independent of the executive[12]. Discretionary life sentences therefore fall into two parts:

i.   the relevant part, which consists of the period of detention imposed for punishment and deterrence, taking into account the seriousness of the offence (known as the 'tariff'), which is set by the trial judge in open court

---

11. Home Office, 2000, Prison Statistics England and Wales 1999.
12. 'Having regard to the foregoing, the court finds the detention of the applicants after the expiry of the punitive periods of their sentences is comparable to that at issue in the Van Droogenbroeck and Weeks cases – the factors of mental instability and dangerousness are susceptible to change over the passage of time and new issues of lawfulness may thus arise in the course of detention. It follows that at this phase in the execution of their sentences, the applicants are entitled under Article 5(4) to take proceedings to have the lawfulness of their continued detention decided by a court at reasonable intervals and to have the lawfulness of any re-detention determined by a court'. (At para. 76)

ii.   the remaining part of the sentence during which the prisoner's detention will be governed by considerations of risk to the public, which is decided by the Parole Board[13].

The trial judge has to indicate reasons for reaching his or her decision as to the length of the tariff. The period should be between one-half and two-thirds of what would have been the appropriate determinate sentence, since this parallels the parole rules for those sentenced to more than four years' imprisonment, who will be released on parole at some point between the one-half and two-third point in the sentence (*R v M (Discretionary Life Sentence); R v L [1999] 1 WLR 485*). The period itself may be the subject of an appeal (D (1994) 16 Cr App R 564).

The new procedures were introduced by section 34 of the Criminal Justice Act 1991[14]. The Parole Board considers the release of discretionary life sentence prisoners in panels known Discretionary Lifer Panels, whose procedures are governed by sections 28–34 of the Crime (Sentences) Act 1997, and by the Parole Board Rules 1997 (SI/1997), issued under s32(5) of the Criminal Justice Act 1991[15]. The Rules develop the legal framework under which Panel hearings operate: the Chairman of the Parole Board appoints the three members of the panel, including a person 'who holds or has held judicial office', who acts as chairman (Rule 3). A letter, dated 1 September 1992, was sent to the Chairman of the Parole Board from the then Home Secretary suggesting criteria for selecting panel members. The Chairman was to be a judge: a High Court judge where cases involve terrorist offences, the attempted murder or wounding of a police or prison officer, the sexual assault or mutilation and killing of a child (i.e. in the same incident), serial rape, manslaughter following release from prison on a previous manslaughter sentence, or offences giving rise to multiple life sentences. Otherwise a circuit judge or recorder was to chair proceedings. The second member was generally to be a psychiatrist, though if there was conclusive medical evidence that no serious concern existed about the prisoner's state of mind at the time of the offence or subsequently during imprisonment, a psychologist or probation officer could be appointed. The third member of the panel was to be a lay member, a criminologist, or a psychologist or probation officer (where he or she was not already the second member)[16].

---

13. See Practice Direction (Imposition of Discretionary Life Sentence) [1993] 1 WLR 223.

14. This has now been replaced by section 28 of the Crime (Sentences) Act 1997, which itself has been amended by the Crime and Disorder Act 1998, Schedule 8. The version currently in force is to be found in Appendix 3.

15. The original Rules were drawn up in 1991–2, and came into force on 1 October 1992, but were amended following the coming into force of the 1997 Act which extended DLP procedures to cover those sentenced to detention during Her Majesty's Pleasure, as well as the new category of 'automatic' lifer sentenced under s2.

16. The letter concluded 'I recognise these criteria will reduce your flexibility in scheduling panels. If they cause too much difficulty, I hope you will let me know.'

The Rules provide that within eight weeks of the case being listed for hearing, the Secretary of State serves on the Board the information and reports specified in the Rules and 'such further information that the Secretary of State considers to be relevant to the case' (Rule 5). However, if the Secretary of State is of the opinion that some part of the information or some reports 'should be withheld from the prisoner on the ground that its disclosure would adversely affect the health or welfare of the prisoner or others', those parts are to be recorded in a separate document and served only on the Board together with the reasons for believing that its disclosure would have that effect (Rule 5(2)). Such information should also be served on the prisoner's representative if he is a lawyer, a doctor or other suitable person (Rule 5(3)).

Within five weeks the prisoner should inform the Board whom he has authorised to represent him or her. Other people may accompany a prisoner to a hearing, subject to the agreement of the Governor (Rule 6). Within 12 weeks of listing, any party wishing to call witnesses must apply to the Board, giving the name, address and occupation of witnesses and 'the substance of the evidence he/she proposes to adduce' (Rule 7). The Chairman of the panel may grant or refuse an application, and must give reasons in writing in the case of a refusal (Rule 7(2)). Within 15 weeks of the case being listed the prisoner must serve his/her own representations on the Board, and any other documentary evidence that he/she wishes to adduce shall be served on the Board and the Secretary of State at least 14 days before the date of the hearing (Rule 8).

The Rules provide that the Chairman of the panel may give, vary or revoke directions for the conduct of the case. By these directions the judge deals with requests for the attendance of witnesses, and they are usually dealt with on paper only, though a preliminary hearing may be held. An appeal from such directions lies to the Chairman of the Parole Board within 14 days (Rule 9).

Except where both parties and the Chairman of the panel agree otherwise, there must be an oral hearing, and the prisoner must notify the Board within five weeks of the case being listed whether he/she wishes to attend (Rule 10). The parties should have at least three weeks notice of the date, time and place for the hearing (Rule 11) and the hearing should be held in private at the prison where the prisoner is detained. The Chairman of the panel may admit such persons on such terms and conditions as he/she considers appropriate (Rule 12).

Rule 13 specifies that the panel shall seek to avoid formality in the proceedings. At the beginning of the hearing, the Chairman is to explain the order of proceedings which the panel proposes to adopt. The parties may hear each other's evidence and put questions to any witness. The formal rules on inadmissible evidence do not apply, but nobody can be compelled to give evidence or produce any document which he/she could not be compelled to give or produce on the trial of any action. After all the evidence has been given, the prisoner is to be given a further opportunity to address the panel. Rule 14 provides for adjournments; and Rule 15 provides that decisions, which may be made by majority, shall be recorded in writing, with reasons, signed by the Chairman of the panel, and communicated in writing to the parties not more than seven days after the end of the hearing.

Any irregularity resulting from a failure to comply with the Rules does not render the proceedings void, but 'the panel may, and they shall, if it considers that any person may have been prejudiced, take such steps as it thinks fit, before determining the case, to cure the irregularity' (Rule 18).

The impact of judicial review on the operation of DLPs

Since there is no appeal from decisions of the Parole Board, the only legal remedy against a decision is by way of judicial review. Since 1992, there have been a large number of applications for judicial review[17], but success is rare, unsurprisingly given that an applicant has to prove either that the Board acted illegally, irrationally or followed irregular procedures[18]. Perhaps the most important message to have come from the Divisional Court is the importance of clear and cogent reasons being given to the prisoner. *R v Parole Board, ex p Bradley* [1991] 1 WLR 134 and *R v Parole Board, ex p Watson* [1996] 1 WLR 906; [1996] 2 All ER 641 are two cases which have been considered by the Court of Appeal[19]. In *Bradley*, Stuart-Smith LJ held that the Parole Board had to apply a test of dangerousness: they had to be convinced that the level of risk which the prisoner presented was 'a substantial risk of further offences dangerous to life or limb, including serious sexual offences'. His analysis went further: 'The Parole Board have to carry out a balancing exercise between the legitimate conflicting interests of both prisoner and public. They must clearly recognise the price which the prisoner personally is paying in order to give proper

---

17. See for example, *R v PB, ex p Telling* (6 May 1993); *R v PB ex p Gittens* (26 Jan 1994); *R v SSHD, ex p Douglas* (15 June 1994); *R v PB, ex p Lodomez* (4 May 1994); *R v SSHD and the PB, ex p Norney* (1995) 7 ALR 861; *R v SSHD, ex p Bushell* (14 Dec 1994); *R v SSHA, ex p Edwards* (20 March 1996); *R v Parole Board, ex p Davies* (25 Nov 1996); *R v Parole Board, ex parte McIntyre* (2 December 1997); *R v SSHD, ex p Murphy* [1997] COD 478; *R v PB, ex p Hirst* (21 October 1997).

18. The supervisory jurisdiction of the High Court is based on the common law powers of courts to keep bodies within their jurisdiction. Thus a decision-maker's decision must not be biased, it must not be vitiated by illegality, irrationality or procedural impropriety. These heads of judicial review were explored in the classic GCHQ case (*Council of Civil Service Unions v Minister for the Civil Service* [1985] AC 374).

19. *Bradley*, although decided on the pre-1991 rules, remains relevant.

effect to the interests of public safety. They should recognise too that it is a progressively higher price. Accordingly, the longer the prisoner serves beyond the tariff period, the clearer should be the Parole Board's perception of public risk to justify the continued deprivation of liberty involved' (at p 146).

The Court of Appeal considered the function of the Parole Board in recall cases in Watson, whose discretionary life sentence had been imposed in 1975 for various sexual offences. He had been released in 1993, but recalled in March 1994 because of probation service concern over his association with young men and his cohabitation with a 17-year-old. The Lord Chief Justice upheld the Parole Board's decision to recall, confirming that, in the absence of express statutory provision, the Board should apply the same test on recalls as it does on earlier reviews. The House of Lords has yet to consider DLP procedures[20].

An example of the role played by judicial review is provided by a recent case in which the Divisional Court quashed the decision of the Parole Board. In R v Parole Board, ex p Robinson (Divisional Court, 28 July 1999), Robinson had pleaded guilty to the manslaughter of his 15-month-old step-daughter in 1969 and had been sentenced to life imprisonment. He was released on licence in 1980, but in March 1984, following conviction for an offence of obtaining child benefit (£13) by deception, his licence was revoked. He has remained in prison ever since, having spent 26 out of the last 30 years in prison. In June 1998 a DLP concluded that there was no evidence of significant risk to life or limb, and that such risk as there was 'should be susceptible to management within a structured release plan'. This was despite the evidence of Robinson's probation officer that he was a risk, and that she had not been able to prepare a release plan because several probation hostels had refused to accommodate him. As the judge who chaired this panel said in evidence, 'the panel considered that the applicant had been let down by the Avon Probation Service and we were determined to achieve his release'. However, the Probation Service maintained its original position that a structured release plan involving hostel accommodation was essential and since no hostel was available, no plan was achievable. The panel therefore adjourned the case for 28 days for the formulation of an appropriate structured release plan. In August 1998 a second panel refused to direct his release because it was not 'satisfied that it is no longer necessary for the protection of the public that the prisoner should be confined'. The Divisional Court held that on the facts of this case, the second panel were not entitled to re-open the question of risk. There was nothing preliminary or provisional about the first panel's decision: the adjournment was not for reconsideration of risk but merely to facilitate release. Justice to the prisoner required that

---

20. R v SSHD, ex parte Stafford [1998] 4 All ER 7, which concerned the Home Secretary's role in the release of mandatory life sentence prisoners, may be relevant.

the decision as to risk had to be regarded as final and conclusive, subject only to the Secretary of State demonstrating that it was fundamentally flawed or pointing to a supervening material change of circumstances.

The discretionary lifer process in practice

Within the Prison Service, most life sentence prisoners are managed by the Lifer Management Unit (LMU) of the Sentence Management Group (SMG)[21] in the Directorate of Regimes, although the movement of Category A prisoners remains the responsibility of Category A Section within the High Security Directorate. Male prisoners who are not Category A will be allocated to one of the six main lifer centres on receipt from a local prison: Wakefield, Long Lartin, Wormwood Scrubs, Gartree, Swaleside and Brixton. Women life sentence prisoners go to Durham or Bullwood Hall; young male lifers go to Aylesbury, Moorland or Swinfen Hall.

This initial allocation to a main lifer centre should happen within 28 days of sentence, and the initial Life Sentence Plan should be completed within three months of arrival in that prison. A Confidential Summary Dossier is compiled in LMU and copied to the prison. This forms the basis of the risk assessment, which is used throughout the sentence to determine whether or not the lifer is safe to release. Progress reports (F75s) are compiled after three years, and then every two or three years until the first review. In the meantime, the Life Sentence Plan is kept under annual review in the prison where the prisoner is held (although it would appear that these two frameworks for sentencing planning are not well integrated[22]). LMU also has other responsibilities which may be highly influential on the later parole decisions:

- transfers of prisoners for operational reasons or following incidents of bad behaviour
- escorted absences for Category C prisoners who are allowed to visit a local town
- temporary release on facility and resettlement licence for lifers in open condition.

---

21. previously the Adult Males, Parole and Lifer Group (AMPLG).
22. See *Lifers: A Joint Thematic Review by Her Majesty's Inspectorates of Prison and Probation* (Home Office, 1999c), Chapter Six.

Although a prisoner is not legally entitled to a DLP until he or she has served the tariff part of the sentence, three years (or three and a half years) before tariff expiry, a review will take place which consists of a paper review. This review is conducted by the mandatory lifer panel which meets at the Parole Board on Friday mornings. The purpose of this review is to allow the Parole Board to recommend suitable prisoners for open conditions at this stage so that they may be considered for release on tariff: it is therefore a key but invisible stage in the DLP process.

The second review will normally take place by a DLP on, or shortly after, tariff expiry. It is the Lifer Review Unit (function to ensure that the reviews are carried out on time and to prepare the dossier of papers for the Parole Board. About 25/26 weeks before the start of a quarter, LRU sends to the Parole Board a list of cases to be considered during that quarter. This is the formal referral to the Parole Board required by s28(6)(a) of the 1997 Act (see Appendix 1). Soon after that a provisional timetable is made and panels are arranged. Dossiers are received by the Parole Board about 15 weeks before the hearing, and the Parole Board secretariat then chase solicitors for witness applications and LRU for late reports. Soon afterwards, the panel secretary forwards dossiers to the judge, with a suggested timetable, forms for directions on witness applications, observer requests and Secretary of State's representation (provided the Secretary of State's view has been received), with a covering letter highlighting lack of reports and other relevant issues. About four weeks before the hearing, the panel chairman returns his/her direction forms, duly completed. The panel secretary then takes the necessary steps to complete the preparations, and about three weeks before the hearing sends the dossier to the other panel members. Final arrangements are then issued to members, representatives, witnesses, LRU and the prison.

Between October 1992 and June 1999, 1,271 cases were considered and completed by DLPs, with an average of around 200 cases per year[23].

Table 2.3 shows the outcomes from cases heard during that period:

---

23. Figures supplied by LRU. This number will increase significantly following the introduction of automatic life sentences in the Crime Sentences Act 1997.

Table 2.3:   Outcomes of DLP hearings 1992–1999

DLP Decisions 1992–1999		
Directed for release	216	(17%)
Recommended for transfer to open conditions	254	(20%)
Recommended for transfer to PRES/Resettlement	20	(1.6%)
Recommended for transfer to other prisons	150	(11.8%)
Recommended for consideration of specialist treatment	222	(17.5%)
No recommendation or remain in current location	407	(32%)
Recommended for release for deportation	2	(0.2%)
67 prisoners released by DLPs have been recalled to prison; a recall rate of 31% (excluding deportees)		
TOTAL	1,271	

Recalls to prison

The Home Secretary may, if recommended to do so by the Parole Board, revoke a life licencee's licence and recall him or her to prison. He may also revoke the licence of any life sentence prisoner and recall him or her to prison without a recommendation by the Parole Board, where it appears to him that 'it is expedient in the public interest to recall that person before such a recommendation is practicable' (s32 of the Crime (Sentences) Act 1997; Appendix 1). Table 2.4 shows the number of life licences revoked between 1993 and 1999. On the basis of these figures it would appear that 23 per cent (46 of the 200 directed for release during the period) of released lifers have been recalled. The figures do not distinguish those who are recalled for reoffending from those who are recalled simply for 'expediency'. In these cases, the Parole Board will consider the recalled prisoner's case as soon as possible, but on paper only, normally at a Friday morning mandatory lifer panel. The prisoner, who will have been informed of the reasons for his or her recall, may make written representations to this panel. Unless the panel recommends release, having considered the case on the papers, a full DLP will take place in the prison where the prisoner is within the next few months. The criteria for release are then the same as for any other discretionary life sentence prisoner.

Table 2.4:   *Number of life licences revoked* [24]:

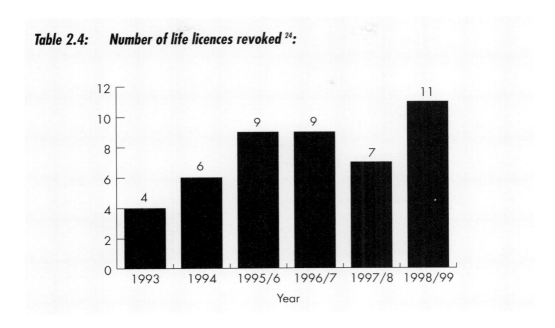

Summary

The *Thynne* decision forced a fundamental change in the decision-making process for the release of discretionary life sentence prisoners. This chapter has set out the formal framework for the operation of DLP's, as it exists 'in the books'. The remainder of our report explores how well this decision-making process operates in practice. Around 200 cases per year have been decided. Our preliminary figures show that in making its decisions on release, panels are also making a significant number and range of other recommendations, including their statutory recommendation on transfer to open prison. In 32 per cent of cases considered between 1992-1999, no recommendation was made. Given the very thorough and resource-intensive system of review we are about to describe, is this efficient? Our introductory chapter has illustrated the cautious nature of decision-making in these cases: in 1998/9, DLP's directed release in only 26 cases. During the same year, licences were revoked in eleven cases. One of our key questions in this report is how satisfactorily the process introduced in 1991 is achieving its aims, whether those aims are clear and whether the continued detention of post-tariff discretionary life sentence prisoners is adequately and regularly reviewed.

24. Taken from Parole Board Annual Report 1998/99. The figures in this table vary from those in Table 2.3, which are based on LRU figures. LRU figures suggest 67 of the 216 prisoners released in 1992–9 were recalled: the Parole Board figures suggest that 46 of the 200 prisoners directed for release between 1993–9 had been recalled. Reasons for this disparity may be that licensees can be re-released without a hearing; that not all recallees make representations; and that the periods covered in the tables may differ (i.e. recalls in one year may not be heard by a panel until the next).

Part two   Research findings

"Given the importance of decision-making in the operation of law, the lack of research explicitly focused on the question of how decisions are made is surprising. Furthermore, a great deal of work which has been carried out has relied upon quantitative methodologies which, in conjunction with an artificial conception of human judgement, have tended to do violence to the inherent complexities involved in making decisions in legal settings…There is little conception, in the first place, of decision-making as process, a highly subtle, shifting, dynamic matter. Second, there is little conception of the problematic nature of the information which is the raw material for the decision. There is, third, little conception of the broader constraints within which decision makers operate: ideological, symbolic, socio-political, economic, organisational and interactional. Finally, there is little conception of the interpretative work in which decision-makers engage and the meaning of matters defined as relevant." (Hawkins, K, *Thinking About Legal Decision-Making*, 1983:8).

3   The discretionary lifer panel process observed

"It is time now to worry about something that has been implicit throughout the discussion of methodology ... those mysterious procedures by which you transform what you see and hear into intelligible accounts" (Michael H Agar, *The Professional Stranger*, 1980: 189).

Introduction

In this Part, we try to provide an intelligible account of what we have collectively observed to be the essence of the DLP process. We set out in detail all stages of the decision-making process that we have observed, with one exception. Although we were not asked to consider the pre-hearing stage, we include here a brief account of this stage (as we have understood it) for completeness. We begin by offering two composite portrayals, drawing on our observations of over 40 panel hearings. We outline the 'typical' sequence of events in two types of establishment (an open and a closed prison), the social setting and the main characters involved.

In this chapter and the next, our aim is to describe as fully as we can how the process of decision-making operates. What are the ways in which 'the knowledge that is treated as the raw material for decision' is socially organised? What forms of negotiation and interaction occur? What techniques of simplification, presumption, characterisation and patterning take place[25]? Are decision-makers sceptical about some participants' accounts and not about others'? How is credibility judged? We present our data in full in these two chapters, then we shall attempt to answer some of these evaluative questions in our concluding chapter.

After our two summary accounts, we raise two important broad questions about what it is that panels do: what is the nature of 'the decision' they make; and how do they set about assessing risk? We return to the beginning in Chapter 5 and set out in more detail aspects of the decision-making process. All of the following accounts draw on our observations and on the interviews and other materials gathered during the course of the research.

---

25. A particularly helpful article by Keith Hawkins on legal decision-making shaped our thinking at the analysis stage (Hawkins, 1983). Other sources which we found useful as we sifted through our data were Hood and Shute, 1995, and 2000; Bottomley,1990; Coker and Martin, 1985; and Cullen and Newell, 1999.

The DLP process observed

Taking a controlled risk

> In this case the prisoner was recommended for release, from an open prison. The panel were divided to begin with, but finally reached a consensus.

The solicitor arrived first, at 9.15am. He met with his client, then was escorted to a waiting room next to the board room at 10am, where coffee was available. The judge arrived next, followed closely by the independent member and then the psychiatrist. They were served with coffee in the board room. They exchanged pleasantries, and discussed their cases. The judge asked if they could look together at the case of W. 'I have concerns', he said. The psychiatrist agreed. The independent member said 'I have concerns the other way'. They discussed the nature of the offence, and whether the prisoner was a 'sadistic psychopath'. The psychiatrist suggested that they reserve judgement. They commented that his release plan was impressive, and that it would be difficult to justify keeping him in. They agreed that the case was very difficult. 'It will be a great advantage to see him.'

At 11am, the hearing formally began. The prisoner entered, followed by his legal representative, the lifer governor (the Secretary of State's representative) and two witnesses. The judge suggested that a suitable procedure would be to hear the Secretary of State's view, and then the legal representative. The witnesses were to be an independent psychologist for the prisoner and a probation officer. The Secretary of State's representative read out the Secretary of State's view:

> The Secretary of State's view based on the material contained in the dossier is that Mr W presents an acceptable risk for release on life licence. The Secretary of State notes the continued positive views of reporting officers and Mr W's sensible response to the outcome of his last DLP. The comments of the psychologist…ruling out the likelihood of sadistic motives or intent, which was of concern to the previous panel, have also been noted. The Secretary of State notes that Mr W is considered to present a low risk of reoffending and has a sound release plan based on residence at [a] hostel. The Secretary of State considers the additional safeguards relating to curfew, employment and further offending behaviour work to be sensible and that they should be included in the life licence by way of amended and/or additional conditions.

The judge invited the solicitor to start the questions. The solicitor made some opening remarks:

'Thank you. I don't intend to review the terrible facts of these offences. I represented Mr W at his last two panels and there has been a lot of progress.' He then went on to raise the concern the panel may have about 'the possibility of sadism', following the last review. It had arisen 'out of the blue' and therefore had been addressed in the preparations for this hearing. The judge replied: 'There are two points of focus for us. One, the degree of risk, and two, the support programme set up by probation'. From the dossier, the panel had more concerns about the former than the latter.

This set the tone for the subsequent discussion, which concentrated on risk. An expert witness was called and asked to offer advice on the distinctions between sadism and sexual excitement and to discuss details of the prisoner's index offence, with these distinctions in mind. He clearly recommended release on the basis of his own report, subject to further work being carried out on release. The judge remained cautious. The next witness was the prisoner. The judge addressed some remarks to him: 'You have clearly made some effort, but we are concerned about the risk you may present in the future. What do you want to say?' The prisoner replied that he had gained insight into his feelings, his family and his insecurities, had learned to communicate and he did not 'want to devastate people's lives any more'. The psychiatrist questioned him closely on his choice of victims, his motives, his past and present fantasies, and about the effects of his crimes on his victims. He was asked by all the panel members about his view of strict ('onerous') supervision conditions, his employment and leisure plans and his strategies for managing his own risk behaviours. They discussed possible residence in a hostel and possible ways of testing his resolve. He was also asked about his relationships with family members.

The judge remarked that the release plan was good. Then he asked for a break, so that the panel could have a brief discussion. The other participants left the room. The panel discussed the credibility of the expert witness (which was high, because he was 'very practical' and 'makes no guarantees'). They felt that they were being presented with 'a manageable risk'. The independent member in particular felt that unless he was never to be released, there were insufficient grounds to detain him further. The judge wondered whether he should be tested for a little longer. The role of his supervising officer may have been a key factor. They discussed the prisoner's presentation: was it credible? Had he got genuine empathy? Fifteen minutes later, they called the others back in. The home probation officer was called. She gave an impressive, confident and knowledgeable account of the supervision plans, the work to be carried out, and back-up arrangements. The Senior

Probation Officer was called and questioned about his/her own involvement in the supervision of the case. The solicitor asked if he could sum up. He reiterated his case for release, confirming that the release package was thorough and compared Mr W favourably with other cases he had known. The judge remarked that he 'could not have said more, or said it more persuasively'.

It was 1pm. The participants withdrew. The psychiatrist had been persuaded and was satisfied that she had 'put him through the mincer as best I could'. The independent member supported her, adding that his risk may increase 'if he is knocked back'. The judge expressed serious reservations: 'I was a bit concerned about his answer to the questions about alcohol and relationships. He was also a bit thin on risk scenarios.' The other members appealed to the expert witness's view, and to the role of a course on relapse prevention the prisoner would do in the community under supervision. The psychiatrist asked, 'Do you think he ought to be released before he dies? If so, he will never become a stronger case for release, to begin that process of settling into the community, than he is now, will he? Nothing is going to happen in the next two years to improve his chances'. And then, resigned, the judge agreed: 'We've all seen the good results and we're all prepared to be persuaded; we ought to consider release'. 'Then we agree. All three for release.' At 1.10pm, the judge began to draft the reasons. They drafted collectively, discussing each sentence. They each offered corrections, and between them, they considered several possible licence conditions. This process took half an hour. The judge aired a few anxieties about judicial review, if the case were to go wrong. The panel secretary advised about making clear reference to the reasons for release. 'OK? We are agreed? Let's have lunch.'

Seven days later the prisoner received the (very long) decision letter informing him that he was to be released on licence, with conditions. Two weeks after that, he was released to a hostel.

A difficult case

In this case the prisoner was not recommended for release or transfer to open conditions. The panel recommended that the prisoner undertake a specific course, offered by the establishment he was currently in. They recommended an early review, hoping that this would act as an incentive and anticipating a more favourable outcome at the next review, should he receive a positive assessment from the course.

The judge arrived by train and a short walk to the prison. It was a Category B establishment. He was greeted at the gate by officers who were expecting him and others, around 10am. The names of the panel members and legal representative were listed in front of the gate officer, who checked the identity of the judge, asked him to proceed through searching procedures and to leave any unnecessary belongings in the lockers. The searching procedures took a few minutes. The judge was escorted over to the main part of the prison. The panel gradually assembled in a board room (or chapel area) set aside for the day. They were greeted with coffee and biscuits by the parole clerk. The second panel member to arrive was the psychiatrist member. This signalled an exchange of pleasantries, if they had met before, and a few words about the cases they had prepared. The independent member and the panel secretary arrived. Late papers were distributed by the panel secretary. This included the Secretary of State's view. There was a fairly long period of reading of late reports, with a few exchanges. Outside the board room, the lifer governor and the lifer liaison officer were waiting, along with several witnesses and two observers. The legal representative was seeing his client in the visits area.

The panel learned that the second case listed had been deferred. The legal team were not ready and had asked for more time to prepare the case. The panel discussed the case they were about to conduct. They had all read their dossiers thoroughly, and taken extensive notes. The judge thought the prisoner was of very low intelligence; 'We can't do anything for him. He is a sad case. He remains a danger. He needs to be in an institution with 24 hour care. It's all a bit of a mess.' The judge asked the psychiatrist: 'is there anything the psychiatric world can do for him?' The judge and the psychiatrist discussed the case for a few minutes – 'we need to think about future possibilities'. 'He could be considered for Category D. But he would need a lot of input.' The convention was he should go through Category C – 'but I don't see the point in sending him to a Cat C when he hasn't done any work here. The public at large are not at risk – he may be a risk to himself.' Finally, the judge remarked, 'all we can do is assess risk – we can't do anything else with the system. We can only recommend him for D if we think he is no longer a risk and he seems a long way from that. We can't see a way forward at present, from here.' They mentioned the fact that the prisoner was a long way past his tariff, that there might be a problem with drugs, that there had been a recent refusal to co-operate with aspects of the regime and that there were some more courses he might usefully take.

It was 11am. All the panel members were here, and the late reports had been read. 'Are we ready?' asked the judge? 'So, ask them to come in.' The panel secretary left the room and returned with the prisoner, his legal representative, two witnesses, the lifer governor and two observers. They all sat at the table, except the observers who were directed to the seats around the edge of the room. It was a small room, so they were within good visual and hearing distance. The room was silent.

The judge introduced himself and the other panel members to the prisoner. He explained who everyone else was, and sought to put the prisoner at ease. The prisoner was smartly dressed, and nervous. The Secretary of State's representative was invited to read out the Secretary of State's view:

> 'The Secretary of State's view, based on the reports contained in this dossier, is that Mr S is not suitable for release or open conditions.'

> 'The Secretary of State notes that Mr S has completed the Sex Offender Treatment Programme and his participation in the course is recognised as being a significant step towards ultimately reducing risk. He needs to build upon the progress made on the SOTP and complete further work on victim empathy, sexual fantasies, the use of violence and relationship skills. The Secretary of State notes that there is no support among report writers for Mr S to progress to open conditions and agrees that the further work required should be completed in closed conditions.'

The judge invited the Secretary of State's representative to say more. He asked the lifer governor if this prison could offer to do any further work with the prisoner. The lifer governor said 'Yes, there are courses available'. They discussed his recent misbehaviour and its implications. He invited his colleagues on the panel to ask any questions. They declined.

The solicitor was invited by the judge to question the Secretary of State's representative. She began by outlining her aim for the hearing. She understood the limitations of the panel's remit, but intended to urge them to argue for transfer to a Category C prison, to put pressure on the Prison Service to move him on. She challenged both the assumptions made about his level of risk and the need to take the specified courses in Category B conditions. She took the panel through the dossier, raising questions about some of the assumptions in it and highlighting positive remarks. The solicitor questioned the prisoner. Their exchanges were detailed and poignant, and included a dialogue about the offence, his insight into the causes of it and what the prisoner had done to address his own risk. They covered his prison career since the date of sentence and highlighted areas where he had made progress. They anticipated several doubts the panel may have had – tackling the issues of drug use, in and out of prison, his recent behaviour and negative statements made in some reports.

The Secretary of State's representative was invited to question the prisoner. His questioning was challenging, raising evidence of resistance to change. The prisoner tried to be honest, admitted periods of non-compliance and reluctance to take up courses, and defended his current commitment to change.

The judge thanked them. 'Let me ask my colleagues if they have any questions for Mr S.' He invited the psychiatrist to question the prisoner. The psychiatrist asked in more detail about the offence, and about subsequent sexual behaviour. He challenged the prisoner on his ability to control his behaviour and his fantasies. They discussed the content of courses successfully undertaken, and the learning derived from them, his drug use, and his plans for the future. The independent member asked questions about his positive MDT test, his expectations of Category C conditions, his eventual release plans, and his relationships with people outside.

The Secretary of State's representative summed up. He reminded the panel of their duty to protect the public, and the concern about the prisoner's readiness for transfer.

The solicitor summed up. She pointed out that he had now been in prison for 15 years. He was seven years past his tariff. There had been no violence, no sexually threatening behaviour and he had not been a control problem. He had completed several courses successfully, after some delay. It was difficult to see what else he could do at this establishment. It was time to move him on.

The panel had no further questions. It was 1pm. The prisoner, his legal representative and the observers left the room. They were asked to wait outside for the moment.

'Well', said the judge, 'there has been a full ventilation of the case. Anything else you want to explore or shall we send them away? Do we accept the Secretary of State's view? I have a view, but what do you both think?' They discussed their impressions. The psychiatrist leant towards recommending a move, on the grounds that the prisoner was not making progress, that he was not actually showing clear signs of risky behaviour, and that he should be given some hope. The others were more cautious. The judge wanted to move slowly. They would prefer the prisoner to agree to do a specific course he had resisted first. The psychiatrist was persuaded by the others, but defended an early review. They agreed. The panel secretary went to fetch lunch and the judge began to draft their reasons.

The drafting process took half an hour. The judge wrote in silence to begin with, then he read his reasons, sentence by sentence, to the others. They chipped in, making suggestions and additions. The panel secretary intervened – 'you must say why you are not recommending transfer to open', and 'you must give reasons for an early review'. They finished drafting, then broke for lunch.

The prisoner received a letter seven days later. It read as follows:

> The Crime (Sentences) Act 1997 requires the Parole Board to direct your release only if it is satisfied that it is no longer necessary for the protection of the public that you be confined. The panel of the Board who considered your case on [date] was not so satisfied and has therefore not directed your release at this stage. This decision is binding upon the Secretary of State. The panel considered all of the documents before them, including the statement made by yourself, the evidence of [witness] and the submissions made by your legal representative, and Mr X representing the Secretary of State at the hearing. In reaching its decision the panel took particular account of the findings and conclusion of the Sex Offender Treatment Programme you attended, together with the report of [Y]. The panel also noted that you refused to see the [prison] psychiatrist. The panel took the view that you are now showing signs of slow progress and express the hope that this will continue: this will best be achieved by attending appropriate courses on thinking skills and sexual offending available in closed conditions. In the meantime, you remain dangerous and an unacceptable risk. That is the conclusion reached in all the most recent reports, with the exception of [Y's], and with these reports the panel agrees. The panel recommend that your case be reviewed in 12 months because this period would be sufficient for the required work to be completed. This would give you an opportunity to demonstrate that you are willing to make progress.

*   *   *

We were asked to consider the quality of decision-making by panels at hearings. The criteria by which 'quality' may be judged are multiple. We have considered procedural fairness (process), substantive fairness (outcome), the quality of the social practices that occur, the roles played by participants, the particular composition of the panel and the appropriateness, independence and effectiveness of the oral hearing as a mode of decision-making. We were also asked to consider efficiency. The key themes that emerged from our observations then, were: fairness, the nature and practice of risk assessment, the role of caution, the objectives of the hearing and the roles played by participants, individually and as a panel. Finally, we consider whether improvements can be made to the decision-making process.

Before we consider the typical procedure of a DLP hearing, we need to explore two important questions: what is 'the decision' panels are making; and how do they set about assessing risk?

The decision

What is 'the decision'? The key decisions are whether to release or recommend a transfer to open conditions and/or recommend an early review. This decision rests on a prior decision taken, often rather implicitly, about risk. This in turn rests upon a myriad of decisions taken about the apparent facts of the case. In practice, many other decisions are made alongside these key issues of a) risk and b) direction, and panels may spend more time discussing *extra-curricular* decisions like whether or not the prisoner should undertake a specified course. The main decision made by the panel (whether to recommend release or transfer to open) is gradually formulated throughout the process, starting with preliminary judgements made upon reading the dossier. The type of decision being made (release or transfer to open), and the balance of probabilities for or against, influence the way in which panels approach their task. So panels are making decisions about quite different outcomes (release, transfer to open, or other possibilities), which rest on prior decisions or judgements about risk and in cases of very different levels of complexity (where there is poor understanding of the index offence, contradictory evidence, sudden changes of circumstances, etc.). These are extremely difficult decisions to make.

Perhaps easiest of all is the decision to release from open conditions, where this has been recommended by all report writers, including the Secretary of State. In this case, the panel still have a decision to make, but they are really endorsing a clear view indicated throughout the dossier, subject to satisfactory release plans:

> Judge: Let's cut through some of the formalities. We have all read the documents. The hearing was deferred before because the home probation officer was not available as a witness. You are pushing on an open door. But we want to satisfy ourselves as to the conditions.

The panel are carrying out their duty to protect the public, acting as a final hurdle, and requiring the home probation team to prove that supervision arrangements are thorough and appropriate. They have already decided that the prisoner poses a low risk, and they are checking that further work on risk reduction and management will continue and that any future signs of risk will be dealt with as they arise.

Much more difficult is a situation where evidence is contested, risk seems to remain high, panels have different perspectives and report writers have conflicting views. We will look in detail at how panels assess risk and at examples of negotiation and consensus below.

So the moment of decision-making may begin before the hearing and continue until the deliberation, where impressions are confirmed, outstanding concerns addressed and views are exchanged. What takes place during the deliberation is the reaching of a consensus, based on the nature of the discussion, and the resolution or otherwise of issues of concern. The difficulty of this task will depend on how far the oral hearing has influenced panel members and in what direction. The relatively brief discussion which takes place when the formal decision is taken is more likely to concentrate on the implications of the decision (i.e. the pressure to be cautious) than on the evidence itself. We shall consider this process (the deliberation) in more detail in Chapter Four. First we consider how panels assessed risk during a hearing. What did they actually consider when they were assessing risk, and in what ways?

Assessing risk

> I can only rely on the statistics. [They] suggest that we are very effective. In the sense that not a huge number of those people who are released go on to commit serious offences. But you could, I suppose, say that we are being too cautious and therefore there may be people inside who could be released. We can easily ensure that people don't reoffend by only releasing the dead certs. And I would possibly think (speaking for myself…) that I am a cautious person and the risk to the public is my primary consideration. These people haven't got life sentences for nothing. If I err at all, I probably err on the side of keeping them in (judge).

As might be expected, it was unlikely that any one factor would be decisive in Parole Board decision-making for or against release or transfer to open conditions. It was more likely that a consensus would be sought based on the cumulative picture of the prisoner built up from the dossier and throughout the hearing. The degree of risk for decisions to release had to be much lower (and with far more emphasis on post-release supervision and licence conditions) than decisions to transfer to open conditions, where a certain amount of testing was possible. There was a consensus that attitudes towards risk assessment had changed in line with broader developments in the new 'risk industry' (see Sparks, 1997; Nash, 1999).

> It was much more gut feeling, finger in the air stuff ten years ago. I think it's changed for two reasons, really. One is I think that Home Secretary's directions are sharpening things up and the last directions that came out in '96 – specifically headlining protection of the public … And I think actually the training is better now (Parole Board).

There was more knowledge about risk factors, and a very strong link between risk assessments and completion of offending behaviour courses (accredited and otherwise), which we will discuss below. Actuarial models were not used on the whole, largely because no reliable tools exist for this specific population, but also because the essence of Parole Board decision-making was a human process[26]. But panel members generally had a well informed, intelligent and careful approach to their primary task and set out individually and collectively to inquire in detail about those risk factors they had concerns about:

> The nature of the offence, previous convictions, their attitude to it... how much support they have got in the community, how much thought they have given to release plans; probation officer relationship, compliance with medication, if any. Everything, really (psychiatrist).

Panel members would often fairly systematically note risk factors whilst reading the file, and most of these were usually highlighted by report writers anyway. We were often staggered by the honest exchanges between panel members and prisoners about intimate aspects of their behaviour and how this might be linked to risk. One hearing, for example, was conducted along the following lines (from observation notes):

> Judge: Shall we have him in then? Has he been told about the observers?
> Panel secretary: I'll have to tell him now.
> [Prisoner comes in – he is a large, friendly man in prison clothes. He is unrepresented. The judge invites the prisoner to ask the lifer governor any questions, which is unusual.]
> Prisoner to lifer gov: Don't you think my behaviour has changed?
> Lifer gov: His behaviour has changed dramatically. He is a different person since he returned from [psychiatric hospital].
> Judge: Any more questions to the governor?
> Prisoner: No, no. I've got no temper now, I don't touch drugs, or alcohol – I have had negative drug tests.
> Judge: What are you asking us to do today?
> Prisoner: Can I ask [lifer governor] a question?
> Judge: Yes, by all means.
> Prisoner: I read that you'd like to keep me here another 18 months – is that right?

---

26. Some tools were referred to and might be present in dossiers: e.g. the LSIR and the Wakefield risk assessment model; but they were used rarely and inconsistently. During the course of our study, the Parole Board newsletter for July 1999 offered members the Risk of Reconviction Score, an actuarial assessment tool, on disk. Some members were concerned to tell us that they were very uncomfortable that the use of risk predictors would depend on whether panel members used a personal computer.

Lifer gov: That is our recommendation. We said the work required could be done in 18 months.

Prisoner: I agree with that. I agree to work on offence-related work, but only on a one-to-one basis. The staff have been brilliant. I have not started a course yet – I wanted to wait until the panel had decided. I am on enhanced.

Judge: Yes. That really shows how much you have changed.

Prisoner: It's the way staff have looked after me. They have been as good as gold. Most of them didn't know me before. I was mentally ill before I left here – I had bad feelings, it has gone on for years. The medication has just worked, it's brilliant. It keeps me on an equilibrium. I know my risk factors are lifestyle, relationships, anger and alcohol. I'm working on those now.

This compliant prisoner, who had learning difficulties, was asked about his habit, noted in his reports, of wearing women's clothes. His instant and serious reply was: 'Yes. I like to wear women's clothes. But that's not criminogenic.' This wholesale adoption of risk assessment language illustrated the awareness all participants had of the central role played by risk assessment and the way in which risk was considered.

There were some broad distinctions made in the approach panels adopted between prisoners who had offended very early (who became HMPs) and offenders who had longer careers of violence; offenders convicted of sexual and aggravated violent offences and others (repeat fire setters, for example); and prisoners who had learning difficulties or who seemed to lack insight and others who were more able to discuss and think about their own behaviour. Panels were assisted by good psychologists' reports, particularly if the reports were linked to work being carried out. This depended on each establishment's resources:

[We] do risk assessment work [here], which will be based on collecting data from files, from interviews with the prisoner, from reports from other staff, identifying areas that seem to be contributing to the risk of reoffending. If there's work to do then we'll try to do intervention work to increase their insight, increase their anger management strategies … At the end of that, write a report in F75 format for a Discretionary Lifer Panel, which very, very clearly makes statements of 'this is their current risk of reoffending, this is what needs to be done to reduce that risk, these are the things that might increase that risk' and then a very clear statement of recommendation (psychologist).

Risk assessment (even by expert psychologists) is of course an inexact science and we were very aware of the difficulties and dangers of the task. Even highly experienced psychologists working in prisons were cautious about their conclusions:

[How do I assess risk?] …With dice! Right well. You get your case. You read everything that you can get your hands on … in terms of social history, previous offending, index offence, behaviour in prison. You speak to staff that have written reports previously, or currently working with the person. You then go and see your prisoner and to do a risk assessment. I would normally expect to do a minimum of four interviews and that would be if I was really being pushed to produce a report, I'd try and do sort of four, I know sometimes I've done less but that's not a happy position for me to be in, that would be for practical reasons. So what I would do is go and see a prisoner and to start with, you'd do all the usual things you do in interviews in terms of gaining consent and stressing the limits of confidentiality, informed consent and explain to the prisoner what the actual process is going to be and then what I would normally do is, at that point start doing social history from the prisoner, get their account of their life and then possibly in the next interview I'd go through pre-convictions and what I'd be interested in is the context to the convictions and the distal and proximal antecedents in terms of thoughts, feelings and behaviour and I would try and get all those things into a drawing, either in my head or sometimes on paper, a functional analysis of the offence and for the pre-cons and for the index offence as we went along. So do all of that and then what I would do is go back and start focusing on what their awareness is. This would be very much from my head really, I'd focus on what their awareness is of what actually contributed to their offending. Identify some of those and then start trying to work out what their level of insight is into how likely such things are to happen again and what might reduce the likelihood of them happening. And I would want to very clearly have ideas that they have insight into what we are talking about, are they able to identify clear reasons for how things aren't going to happen again and that might be looking at skills and strategies for developing things, it might be looking at problem solving, it might be looking at sort of an awareness of context. A lot of prisoners will go for the, 'it was just one off, it was my wife, I'm not going to get married again', but that's ignoring a lot of the issues about actually dealing with relationships, so I broaden it out (psychologist).

Lifer governors and others were likewise at once encouraged by modern knowledge and training on techniques of risk assessment but also anxious about a managerialist or mechanical approach:

[How do I assess risk?]… As someone very sad and brainwashed into Prison Service procedures I think of it as being in component parts and how the life sentence plan breaks it down into risk factors…you think of it on two levels. You have a general feel from how you've read the whole evidence, you have an immediate reaction to that and a general overview of whether or not you feel that as a whole that prisoner is likely to reoffend. But in terms of preparing for processes, how I would present that would be in component parts with specific points about specific areas of risk. Particularly thinking about situations and feelings and actions that are likely to lead to the offending rather than the eventual offending (lifer governor).

The risk being assessed was both of the likelihood of offending and the severity of any likely offence. Prisoners were on the whole aware of what mattered:

[The main objectives?].. to see that if you are guilty that you show sufficient remorse, sympathy, empathy and that you are fully aware of the consequences of the offence, insight, the consequences of any further offences that may cause recall... to make sure that courses are helping to address things...I have done the Men Without Violence course (prisoner).

This interpretation of the main objectives of DLPs was similar to that given by panel members:

The main objectives...it's only by hearing straight from the inmate himself the extent to which he's changed, the extent to which he can modify his attitudes, the extent to which he's looked at the underlying practice behind the original offence, and it's only then you can begin to make any realistic assessment of risk (independent member).

Although risk assessment was the main task, the question of risk management often formed part of the overall judgement of the panel:

That raises the line between risk assessment and risk management, because if somebody's got a lousy probation officer, you are going to be less willing to release them, aren't you? (judge).

As several respondents pointed out, the fact that a prisoner is recalled does not necessarily mean that the original decision to release was wrong. Breakdown in supervision arrangements or in their overall management in the community could lead to recall associated with substantially increased perceived risk. We will discuss the significance of release arrangements later.

Factors for movement

What the Parole Board were looking for in prison was evidence of change. Some insight into the offence, evidence of offending behaviour work successfully undertaken, and realistic release plans were the primary factors considered. A realistic release plan would usually entail some stable living arrangement and employment plans. After these primary factors, the quality of supervision was significant. Relationships with family were not always significant, as many of the prisoners whose cases we observed had lost contact with families, or their offence had involved a family member. Occasionally, 'unsuitable' or 'turbulent' or newly formed relationships were scrutinised in order to assess risk and the potential contribution to risk made by relationship patterns. Some contact with a family member was usually seen as a positive indication.

Behaviour in prison was seen as significant in fairly specific ways: a co-operative attitude was taken to be an indication of maturity, as was a willingness to take responsibility for the offence (accept the punishment) and take positive steps to live a more law abiding life. Engagement in education (particularly leading to qualifications) and in work was often regarded as a good indicator of risk reduction, but successful completion of offending behaviour courses was seen as more important (and was more commonly raised).

Factors against movement

Attitude and behaviour were crucial factors in the assessment of risk. If prisoners' attitudes were regarded as antisocial or their behaviour uncontrolled, they were often judged to pose an unacceptable risk. Involvement in serious disciplinary offences or drug use was regarded as a bad sign. Evidence of behaviour reflecting the index offence (usually indicating violence) was carefully considered, sometimes with some speculation (in a process described as 'constructing a career as a deviant'; Hawkins, 1983[27]). Where the index offence was extremely violent or (for example, sexual violence, or what some judges referred to as 'nasty killings' as opposed to outburst killings), considerable time was spent during the hearings on these features of a prisoner's behaviour. This would often include detailed interrogation about insight, fantasies, impulses and strategies for control.

We developed a list of factors mentioned often during the pilot stage of our study, and then raised these with all of our interviewees in order to assess whether risk decisions were made

---

27. 'Time is very elastic when careers of deviance are constructed. It can be stretched to extreme lengths in certain cases to embrace items which are seemingly trivial' (Hawkins 1983: 123).

more or less systematically and consistently. We were also able to form some judgement about this from our observations of the hearings and the deliberations. Did various risk factors carry the same weight for most people?

The significance of the tariff

The tariff (the 'punitive' portion of the sentence) was of huge significance to prisoners and their legal representatives:

> A DLP isn't only about release. They are about release at an appropriate point in the sentence ... The minute someone is over tariff they are being detained under preventative powers and not punitive powers and that's why I think it's all wrong that you are asking someone to prove that they are not a risk, which is very difficult... They've served their punishment and the Home Office should have to prove that they are a risk rather than the other way round (legal representative).

This raises a key 'burden of proof' issue to which we return in Chapter Six. It was also argued that any time served beyond tariff had to be (increasingly strongly, they felt[28]) justified by strict criteria of unacceptable levels of risk. To those assessing risk, the relationship was less clear and many thought it was irrelevant to the task of assessing risk. If anything, long periods of time spent beyond tariff indicated a high level of risk[29]. Prisoners were better placed for release if by the time their tariff expired they were in Category C accommodation, but most were not. What the sentencing judge intended when setting the tariff was difficult to ascertain. Often, there was a view expressed at the trial that the circumstances and motives of the offence were unclear and that the offender's dangerousness was impossible to predict. The judge was handing over that task to experts, and postponing it to a later date. Most people agreed that prisoners who served many years beyond their tariff needed to be carefully reviewed; there was a clear distinction between the tariff part and the continually reviewable risk portion of the sentence:

---

28. The 'anxious scrutiny' test: see, for example, Stuart-Smith LJ in R v Parole Board, ex p Bradley (1991) 1 WLR 134: 'The Parole Board .. must clearly recognise the price which the prisoner personally is paying in order to give proper effect to the interests of public safety. They should recognise too that it is a progressively higher price. Accordingly, the longer the prisoner serves beyond the tariff period, the clearer should be the Parole Board's perception of public risk to justify continuing the deprivation of liberty involved' (at p 146); or David Wood, 1988. We shall return to this in our conclusions.
29. But this carries 'self-fulfilling prophecy' dangers.

You're still assessing risk and you see, what happens is that the judge may see what happened as a terribly serious matter, but he is not so certain what the risk is. So he'll set a low tariff so that the parole board will at an early stage review him and see if he can be released. And that sort of chap may well, 20 years later, still be there because he's still a risk (judge).

Most respondents felt 'the tariff hasn't much meaning at this stage' (lifer governor):

No. It is originally but I don't think it's related to assessing risk in the sense that it's far more important that they've actually admitted responsibility for what they've done, and they've done some offence-related work (independent).

I don't think it matters. The question is, is this prisoner, at this point in time, a risk to the public? (LRU).

As prisoners reach their tariff, more interest is shown in release plans and offence-related work. Those who remain in prison a long way beyond tariff are seen as those who 'lack insight', fail to take courses, or:

...don't recognise that they've got to not just put the time in, they've actually got to consider lifestyle, the way they operate and all that sort of stuff – anger management, relationships with women, all that sort of stuff (LRU).

This required behaviour takes a certain skill, however, and not all prisoners had those skills, or were motivated to develop them. There were also difficulties with the timing of offence-related work in relation to the tariff, as prisoners with long tariffs were caught between starting offence-related work early, and then being accused of coasting years later, and losing the benefits once courses were completed.

Security classification

Security classification was seen as more relevant, because it normally represented (or was held to represent) something significant about the behaviour of the prisoner:

How can you assess risk in high security conditions? You can to a degree but you can't assess risk for going out as completely as you can if someone's in Category D conditions. And presumably if they are still on the book, it's because people are still thinking they are dodgy (psychiatrist).

It's not an indicator of risk *per se*, but it can be a proxy for risk (psychiatrist).

However, panels often do not know why prisoners are kept in higher security categories or how the process of recategorisation works and cannot comment on its appropriateness. Security classification was perceived as linked to 'progress' ('it can give you an indication of where they are'). Some respondents were aware of the dangers of reading too much into security classification (as it may be an indicator of the availability of prison places or the risk of escape rather than the risk of reoffending). There was a general expectation that prisoners would move down the categories one stage at a time and be released from Category D.

Panels had an accepted code for recommending a move to a lower category prison ('a progressive move'), and some were more explicit (one or two considered recommending the precise establishment and the course to be taken).

Behaviour in prison

There was probably more variation on this 'risk factor' than on many of the others between panel members, some of whom were relatively sympathetic about the difficulties of life in prison, and so were sceptical about how far minor drug use, minor adjudications and even major 'run ins' and episodes of non co-operation could be taken to reflect risk of reoffending[30]:

> Yeah I do look at that... I can't get worked up because someone has had a joint, even if they were drunk when they committed the offence. You know prisons are a difficult place to be. But yes, I suppose with paedophiles ... who have indulged in grooming behaviour with their victims and then you get wonderful reports from education ... and you find yourself thinking this guy has done the same with the education department, you know – kind of seduced them into their way of thinking. There are other times when I would look at behaviour in prison as a response to the particular prison if I know the prison. So, it's a qualified yes, really – it's not just if they are a nice prisoner they are OK (psychiatrist).

Most panel members however regarded behaviour in prison as an indicator of risk, particularly non co-operative behaviour, behaviour leading to adjudications and positive drugs tests, and resistance to offending behaviour courses. Current behaviour was explored

---

30. We shared their concern about the number of prisoners who had developed their drug habits in prison.

to assess 'levels of stability' (independent). There is some evidence that (specific) behaviours in prison and subsequent behaviour in the community are linked to some degree (Clarke et al,1993), and some panel members were aware of this link and looked for evidence of specific behaviours (often related to the use of alcohol and drugs, the use of violence, anger control and sexual behaviour) being manifested in prison. It was understood that prisoners should be tested in less constrained environments as they progress through their prison career, so that they gradually learn to control their own behaviour rather than having it controlled:

> I think that [prison behaviour] is very important. Particularly...relationships with staff and other inmates...I think showing respect to other people, that's a start. The way a man deals with disappointment. There are some issues, of course, that are irrelevant. There's a huge issue with prisoners who can't get out of [the habit of] dealing with things themselves. And I think it's that inability to deal with things that are beyond their control rather than by smashing up is some indication as to how far they've got. Most of the guys that we've got are pretty violent offenders as a rule and they obviously need to demonstrate they are in control of their tempers (governor).

Some respondents argued that bad behaviour was an indicator of risk, whereas good behaviour in prison was not an indication of low risk. Panel members complained that prison staff writing reports tended to 'be very impressed by good behaviour and ignore other aspects of risk' (psychiatrist):

> I think a clean and tidy cell and a nice cup of tea is given too much of a positive weighting (psychologist).

Compliance with the sentence plan was generally seen as a positive indicator, but most would see prison behaviour in the context of other factors, depending on the nature of the offence and whether relevant issues were likely to emerge in prison.

Some panel members wished they had adjudication details available in the dossier. Others tried to recognise that 'the odd flare up' was only human, 'because it's showing that there's normal blood flowing through the veins' (independent). Prisoners were often frustrated by constructions made about prison behaviour and felt unfairly treated when apparent misunderstandings counted against them:

> I refused an MDT...it was presented as though I was refusing a test because I had drugs in my system not because I was making a protest about a different issue, and I

think I did point out that the governor accepted what I had to say about it and it's reflected in the fact that I got a caution. But...I found the way that she [the Secretary of State's representative] summed up, she included it again, but emphasised the fact that a refused [MDT] test often indicates trying to hide the fact that you're on drugs. It just wasn't the case. But I didn't feel it come across (prisoner).

There was a feeling among those prisoners we spoke to that prison life encouraged or required behaviours others saw as 'risky':

...[P]art of the problem is prison, and if prison is part of the problem, then how can more prison be the answer? I did try to explain a bit about how I don't feel that I am as mature at thirty-[something], as a thirty-[something] year old is outside, and that's true of many people in prison; it kind of stunts your maturity... And there's lots of people that have started off their sentence that display perpetual immature behaviour, like I did...Obviously that's the wrong way to do it, but it's understandable inasmuch as the length of time I've been in, that's how we do it, that's the tried and tested method for people like me to get our point across (prisoner).

Offending behaviour courses

They're the linchpin (lifer governor).

There was universal recognition that offending behaviour courses (and in most cases, their successful completion) were a requirement before prisoners would be considered for a progressive move. It was tempting for panels (and report writers) to regard attendance on a course as shorthand for risk reduction, and we were relieved to hear and see panel members taking a more critical approach to the role of courses in reducing risk. There were observations about the rigid nature of accreditation requirements, about the superficial nature of some courses, and about the unfairness of patchy availability and long waiting lists. Prisoners assumed that offending behaviour courses were hoops they had to jump through, which caused difficulties when no progressive move was forthcoming. We saw several frustrating exchanges between panels and 'stuck' prisoners who were being required to retake a programme they had taken (often in the same establishment) several years before. They had anticipated a move (as a reward for completing the required course), and might have agreed to take further courses elsewhere, but could not bear to hear panels ask them to 'take it again' because its effects had worn off. Panels varied in the extent to which they asked about the significance and content of courses taken:

…[T]here is so much variation on the information we get, in terms of what they've actually done. It's so varied…but as a principle of course, that's the most important thing, whether they've actually understood what the offence was about and whether they've done anything about it (psychiatrist).

The courses were regarded as important because they were seen as effective in raising levels of insight and providing coping strategies for dealing with temptation. There were sometimes conflicts between the DLP process and the timing of courses – if prisoners were in the middle of a Sex Offender Treatment Programme course when their hearing was due they would sometimes defer the hearing in order to include the course assessment in the process of decision-making. Panel members saw them as important but not on their own; and 'what came out of them' was 'more important than the fact that they've done them':

Yes, if they've done the courses and the courses have addressed some of the problem areas, then fantastic. But I think at the moment, offending behaviour courses are seen as the panacea to all things and I don't agree with that (psychologist).

A willingness to undertake a programme and complete one is a good sign (lifer governor).

There were some prisoners who were unable or unwilling to work in a group (where most offending behaviour courses required group work); there were others who were ineligible (due to learning ability) or who completed them for superficial or strategic reasons ('they've been trained'). Some prisoners saw them 'like exams'. There were risks for those prisoners who did engage seriously that more risk indications would emerge during a course and actually hold up release or indicate more work needed. Courses were emotionally demanding and prisoners felt coerced or blackmailed into doing them:

Interviewer: You might find that a whole sentence concentrating on offence-related work would be a bit too much?

Prisoner: Oh yeah, it would probably drive you nuts. There has to be some release from it.

Likewise prisoners might stay in higher security conditions for longer, waiting to do a course.

Generally, there was a basic faith, despite some reservations, that courses and their assessments were improving, and that appropriate subjects (anger control, relationship violence, and so on) were being addressed. Panel members argued that more systematic information about course content and progress would be helpful to them.

Release plans

This includes the prisoner's work, accommodation and other plans, supervision arrangements and relationships, and these issues formed a substantial part of the discussion at hearings, particularly when the panel were considering release (but also earlier):

> I think that it's absolutely essential for the panel to think about somebody's release in terms of where they are being released to, because the risk that they can present is affected by their release plans, so if you can secure for them a release plan that incorporates some of the risk factors by actually providing protection against it, then even though somebody is relatively more risky than another individual, it may still be safe to release them because the risk can be managed (legal representative).

The perceived quality of supervision was essential, and we noted that prisoners seemed more likely to be released if the home probation officer attended the hearing and laid out convincing supervision plans (but this was not always the case; see section on witnesses, Chapter 5). All of those prisoners who were released during the course of our research had positive recommendations by the home probation officer (see Chapter Four). Panel members were very thorough in their approach to release arrangements:

> [D]oes the release plan adequately address the environmental aspects of risk of reoffending; does it put in place sufficient supervisory nets? (psychiatrist).

> If we've got people who have had a very disruptive, chaotic lifestyle prior to coming in prison, the last thing we want to do is put them back out into a similar context...I think it's very important we make things as stable as possible to give people the best start that we can, given that things are going to be difficult for them anyway (psychologist).

Strong realistic release plans were seen as holding in place the low level of risk achieved, providing a safety net and planning in advance to avoid high risk situations. Prisoners often faced difficulties returning to the area where the offence had been committed or to their families and were often released to a hostel, sometimes in a new area (for example, the area of their resettlement prison, where a job had been found). 'Supervisability' and a good relationship with a home probation officer were important:

Brilliant. Brilliant. She knows all my family. She's been round my house to do reports. She's sat in on bad times with me, and good times with me, and I've been up and down. She knows me, whether I am good or bad; whatever I'm doing she knows me and I felt secure that I could go in there and have a bad day and it would be taken as a bad day, not taken as a raving lunatic (prisoner).

In a recall case in which the prisoner's recall was endorsed, great weight was placed on the supervision arrangements and on the relative merits of work done in a resettlement prison or in the community. The prisoner's home circumstances, his attitude towards supervision and his ability to control his drinking were all considered in detail [from observation notes]:

[pre-hearing discussion]
Psychiatrist: Mrs X [his wife] is not very stable, is she? And his attitude to work is not very good.
Judge: The kids are probably a bit out of control too, reading between the lines. This is my provisional view, and it's unfair to judge before the hearing.
Psychiatrist: His failure to turn up to probation appointments is compatible with the behaviour of a drinker; she seems a bit of a victim, she quickly backed down about the violence.
Judge: She is described as self-reliant and independent, but she has a drink problem – what does that mask?
[They discuss the case, and the various reports – they have all read the papers very well....Later during the hearing, when the home probation officer is called as a witness...]
Legal rep: He has co-operated with probation in the past; he has been less co-operative with you?
Home probation officer: I supervised him in 1997, and now I have taken him on again. This time he was more unsettled. He was in limbo. He was doing casual work, so he didn't keep to his appointments as agreed. When he did come, it was unannounced. I could see he had been drinking, and I couldn't do any relevant work with him. He came in the evenings; we just couldn't look at the issues I was concerned about.
Legal representative: Would you say he has the capacity to co-operate?
Home probation officer: Yes.
Legal representative: You have heard that he would like more involvement? He has asked for better supervisory arrangements?
Home probation officer: 'According to national standards' he should be seen weekly and then fortnightly. It is important that it is at an agreed appointment time. Home

visits are unlikely in the current resource and workload climate.

Legal representative: Can you describe the alcohol package?

Home probation officer: The courses in prison are 'in theory'; the next stage is putting it into practice. If he went to a resettlement prison, he would have to get a job and return to prison in a completely sober state. This programme in the community is about drinking and where to draw the line. It is the course I favour. It is a case of finding what is safe for them. They are aiming to achieve what is safe to drive a car. That way you remain in charge of yourself. He has to take on board these exercises, and the information involved. And comply with National Standards for [Probation] reporting.

In this case there were clear indications that the prisoner had developed a very good relationship with his previous probation officer, who had visited him in his home, and worked with his family and with him on many aspects of his behaviour. He had moved area, and was now faced with a probation officer with whom he did not get on and who he did not see as helpful. The panel were not convinced that he could be released safely. His compliance with the requirements of supervision shortly before his recall had been variable. With a different relationship with his probation officer, he may have been a much better prospect (the same medium level of risk, but a better managed level of risk). There were serious concerns about his drinking, which both he and his wife failed to appreciate. He drank four cans of Guinness regularly, and there was evidence that they fought (sometimes leading to minor violence) under the influence of alcohol. The panel and the prisoner were unable to reconcile their very different perceptions of what was an acceptable amount of alcohol (of what sort) to drink, or what was an acceptable level and manifestation of conflict within a relationship. This failure to agree was interpreted by the panel as 'a poor attitude to alcohol, which incorporates minimisation and resistance to advice from others'. Financial difficulties, stepchildren and working for cash were seen as 'adding to the risk'. Cultural and class differences made this dialogue impossible to resolve. How far the ordinary problems of living could or should be included in risk assessments was a question which taxed us as observers.

The Index Offence (IO)

The circumstances of the index offence and previous offending behaviour were both seen as important in assessing risk:

> Well I look very hard at the original crime and the circumstances of it. What was said at the time…because at that point he was at the most dangerous in relation to

the crime. Then I decide...I suppose I do a sort of mental exercise as to how dangerous or how unpleasant or how sadistic or whatever affective word you want to use about the crime itself...Then I look back at the reports at that time to establish what sort of risk factors it was thought he posed at the time (judge).

Prisoners were rarely allowed to forget the seriousness of their crimes, several years after their tariff had expired:

Interviewer: How did you feel in the days after the hearing?

Prisoner: A little bit better than I was immediately after, like coming out of there, cos I thought like, I'm gonna lose here. I just didn't pick up any positive indicators from the panel. I don't know if you overheard the kind of questions coming from the actual case itself, the murder itself? The judge...he reminded everybody of the brutality of it and it kind of made me think he was more interested in that issue...and I felt kind of disappointed because that's work we'd already covered but now it seemed to me that he was making an issue of it.

Their attitude towards the offence (and towards other people) was an important topic almost always covered in detail by the hearing. The level of insight into the original offence and the likelihood of its repetition were often explored. Panels liked to see prisoners taking responsibility for the offence, and taking positive steps to minimise its recurrence.

Attitude towards the victim, denial and the role of remorse

He does show an element of remorse, but finds it difficult to express in that he has repeated the details of his offence many times over the years. He is very open about the offence and is willing to go into detail. He explains that he went out deliberately to find someone with whom to have sex. He recognises that he used a young girl because it was someone he could exert power over. He also recognises that the girl was very frightened and speaks about her screaming. He said that 'it will affect her for the rest of her life, and I understand why I have to spend a long time in prison' (chaplaincy report, F75).

'Expressions of guilt are important and, though probably necessary for a confident recommendation of release, are not sufficient' (Tidmarsh, 1999).

The victim's view or circumstances were seen as significant in informing licence conditions (such as no contact, residence away from the victim or the victim's family) but not as relevant to risk, or the release decision, unless there had been evidence of further threats or continuing contact. What mattered was that prisoners had understood the effect that their offence had upon the victim(s). Remorse, insight into offending behaviour, victim empathy and willingness to engage in offending behaviour courses were linked in actual assessments of risk, although remorse was difficult to assess, particularly many years after the offence. Panels sought an intellectual and emotional understanding of the seriousness of the offence, but treated it as 'something where you have to build up a picture over time'. There was an operational consensus that expressions of remorse (those perceived as 'genuine') were an important component of 'making progress' in prison (Tidmarsh, 1999) – 'almost a starting point'. There was less consensus about how far a perceived lack of remorse should hold up the release decision[31].

Lack of remorse and denial were seen as particularly significant and inappropriate in cases of sexual crime. Just over a third of imprisoned sex offenders are found to deny their offence compared with eight per cent of non sex offenders (Hood and Shute, 1995). Tidmarsh asks whether this is due to 'fear of persecution by other prisoners' or 'less obvious psychological mechanisms' (Tidmarsh, 1999). There was acknowledgement by several respondents that sex offenders may start their offending careers as victims, and that in these cases 'remorse' is not straightforward. What Tidmarsh calls the 'prognostic relevance of guilt' is unknown[32]. The question of denial of guilt 'has always been a problem for the parole system', and there was evidence that those who deny their offence or show insufficient remorse take longer to achieve release. Many offenders rationalise their offending or minimise their responsibility, and it was interesting to note that those sex offenders who did acknowledge guilt often did so at a late stage. Prisoners found the emphasis on remorse difficult and were not as good as some individuals thought at 'giving an emotional performance':

---

31. *Denial* of the offence is not sufficient grounds to refuse release in law, but is linked in practice to a resistance to take up courses deemed relevant to risk reduction. Where risk is perceived to be low, denial should not be considered. However, refusal to take up courses on the grounds of denial can be an indication of continuing high risk. See *R v Secretary of State ex parte Zulfikar* (1996) COD 256.

32. A recent study evaluating the effects of motivation on a relatively small group of sex offenders participating in a national Sex Offenders Treatment Programme at three establishments concluded that motivation did not influence outcome. The prisoners studied were divided into three groups; those who participated because they wished to address their offending behaviour; and two groups who participated for instrumental reasons; lifers seeking release and other prisoners seeking parole or enhanced privileges. Cognitive distortions were measured before and after participation in the programme and this was taken to be a satisfactory measure of treatment efficacy. 22 out of 31 offenders showed significant reductions in the number of cognitive distortions reported. Motivation was not a factor in treatment outcome (Terry, 1999).

What I am trying to say is that you tend to get a bit cynical and rattle off a few sorries, like I'm reading the football results. I'm not trying to be nasty about it, but I just have to say, 'who have I got to be sorry to this week?'...Prison isn't a remorse place. This is not going to be a nice thing to say, but if you think too much about your offence...you get some people in prison who try and commit suicide... eventually you have to live with what you've done – a bit like a death in the family (prisoner).

In the end, the term 'victim empathy', 'understanding the effect that their actions had on their victims', was preferred to remorse as it was easier to test. We were given examples of prisoners who refused to discuss their offence for years and then gradually came to terms with the enormity of what they had done. This was regarded as a key stage in the reduction of future risk. But there were others who 'regretted the situation they were in', or who 'mentioned their families before the victims', and these sorts of remarks were 'revealing' for panels concerned about risk.

Other factors

Other factors considered by panels as contributing to risk included 'risky relationships' (turbulent relationships, or types of relationships that might be disapproved of – including homosexual partnerships or relationships with large age differences); a prisoner's attitude at the hearing; thoughts and feelings generally; use of time; relationships with staff and with other prisoners; the role of medical treatment (and compliance with it); evidence of learning from their mistakes; general comparisons between behaviour at the start of the sentence and current behaviour; and towards release, and behaviour on home leaves. Sometimes it was difficult for past, static factors to be forgotten or overcome – for example, breaches of supervision requirements, repeat offending, psychiatric diagnoses, and so on. In the end, panel members were sure that there was an 'intuition gradient' in all their decision-making: 'it was just his demeanour', 'I just felt creepy', or 'we were swayed by the personal interaction of the event', 'you have a personal feeling about the individual':

> There has to be gut feeling in the end and that's why you need I suppose people who've got a wide experience of life and of assessing situations (governor).

There were mixed views about whose responsibility it was for prisoners to make progress, attend the right courses, engineer the right treatment and achieve an identifiable reduction in risk. Some prisoners clearly became 'stuck' in the wrong establishment or without sufficient motivation to progress, or found that the sort of help they needed was not available. Sometimes, new courses were introduced which meant that prisoners who thought they were 'on their way out' (and who had 'done everything that's expected of me') would become 'stuck in the system' waiting to do newly recommended programmes, or prisoners 'couldn't handle the course', which disadvantaged them.

Our data was analysed with a view to discerning any notable issues concerning bias. There was no evidence of any overt sexual or racial discrimination in the decision-making. Unfortunately we observed only one hearing involving a female prisoner (another objected to any observers at the panel; we did observe a few female mandatory lifer cases at Friday morning hearings), therefore this did not allow for any direct comparison. The case we observed was held in closed conditions and the prisoner was recommended for a 'progressive move' or hospital.

Of those respondents who did comment on gender issues, there was a consensus that women were particularly 'damaged' and that self-harm, arson, childcare and family responsibilities were significant issues. They were often victims of abuse:

> We get a lot of people here, that as a cry for help, set light to things. How does that play into the wider consideration of risk factors? (Secretary of State's representative).

> Women's cases tend to be a bit like this, a collection of problems together. Hard to see progress (judge).

This made their cases even more difficult to assess. Race and gender issues arose during our observations but panels were normally fairly sensitive to them. In fact we wondered (on the basis of some of our observations) whether the Parole Board sometimes countered the bias of the Prison Service when prisoners seemed to have been held back (for example, in part, for not being able to speak English) and then were swiftly released, against the majority of reports' recommendations. On the other hand, more subtle cultural assumptions were more difficult for the panel to exclude.

We accepted throughout our research period that panels were 'assessing risk'. However, when analysing the results of the research, we questioned whether this is in fact an appropriate way of describing what panels were actually doing. The decision-making, and panels' consideration of specific risk factors, was systematic, but it wasn't standardised or validated. They were using their 'common sense' to balance the various factors. Generally the same factors carried similar weight in different cases. Thus, if the prisoner was in open conditions, the risk factors which carried more weight were release plans and supervision arrangements. If the prisoner was in closed conditions, then behaviour in prison, offending behaviour courses, and the index offence (including his or her insight into it) were more important. This raises questions about the status and range of relevant risk factors as indicators of risk, to which we return in our conclusions. We also witnessed strong opinions and negative judgements about lifestyle and personal characteristics (for example, on promiscuity, homosexuality and living conditions) but it was difficult to unravel the extent that these might have influenced decisions and outcomes.

Summary

This chapter has introduced the nature of the decision-making process and the sort of decision the panel were seeking to make. They were looking at dynamic risk factors (those that change), in the light of often quite severe 'static' risk factors (like the nature of the offence). Despite the clear evidence of subjectivity demonstrated throughout this account of risk assessment, there was some scope for bias to be checked during the deliberations (pre- and post-hearing) because of the composition of the panel, and the need to reach a consensus (see further on this point in Chapter Five). We did observe some panels talking themselves into agreement on the basis of lazily constructed and biased interpretations of evidence, but this occurred infrequently. Recall cases were the most difficult, as sometimes very minor but potentially offence-related behaviour could lead to a return to prison, without any testing of the evidence on which assertions were made.

There seemed to be considerable consistency in those areas of decision-making relating to risk, including the types of risk factors taken into account. There was some danger that articulate, presentable prisoners were more likely to be released than inarticulate less presentable prisoners:

> I mean, all of the people who are released tend to have exemplary records and the people who are not released are the ones who are just bizarre (legal representative).

There was also evidence that prisoners who had 'committed, professional home probation officers' stood a higher chance of achieving release. We shall look more closely at decisions and outcomes (at who was released and who was not) in Chapter Four.

What is less consistent is the choice of norm or standard of risk adopted over time. Panels seemed to avoid discussing levels of risk. It seemed to us that the Board operated with extreme caution, rarely 'taking a considered risk' on the grounds that this may assist in the process of resettlement. We heard several times the lone voice of an individual panel member arguing that 'this man/woman's risk will never be lower. If we do not intend to detain forever, we have to consider release':

> If there's doubt then you've got to err on the side of caution. Now, you might say that's because you as a parole board member don't want too many failures (psychiatrist).

> I do also have at the back of my mind that thing about how many people do we not release...that could have been released? (Parole Board).

This is the problem of 'proving safety' from within a prison environment. Risk assessment was an extremely difficult task. It was carried out thoroughly and 'in good faith', with protecting the public firmly in mind. It was carried out very cautiously, and sometimes without sufficient information of the right type. Being cautious was seen as appropriate, given the nature of the offences considered. There was some feeling that prisoners could be moved (downgraded) between prisons more speedily and less cautiously, but that the decision to release should remain most carefully considered and with a close eye on plans for release and supervision.

4

The main stages of the decision-making process in practice

Introduction

In the last chapter we looked at the operation of the decision-making process by concentrating on the key decision, and at how panels assess risk. In this chapter we explore in more detail the decision in its various stages at the hearing. What 'goes on' during the process, and how do decisions get made? We look briefly at how panel members prepare for hearings and then at the pre-hearing discussions (which we were able to attend), the hearing, the deliberation and the drafting of the reasons in the form of a letter to the prisoner. All of these stages in the decision-making process were observed. We then raise some issues arising from our account: the role of the dossier, the question of deferrals and delays, and the differences between recall cases and 'ordinary' DLP cases. We shall consider the roles played by all the participants in more detail in Chapter Five. However, we start with a few words on the pre-hearing review and the panel's pre-hearing preparation, both crucial stages in the decision-making process.

The pre-hearing review

A few weeks before the hearing, the judge as Chairman received the dossier. The directions he or she could give at this stage were clearly of importance in avoiding deferrals: a strong message from the Chair could ensure that certain hitches would be avoided, that appropriate witnesses were called, and that irrelevant witnesses were excluded. He or she could also direct that the lifer governor should not be the Secretary of State's representative, if his or her report clashed with the view of the Secretary of State[33]. However, since the Secretary of State's view was often not received until shortly before the hearing, this decision was often taken at a very late stage.

---

33. It was clear from our observations that many judges did not see this as a key part of the process. A judge would ask about who the parties were calling as witnesses, even though it had been their role to give directions for witnesses. Another said, 'I've never called a witness. I agree witnesses.' These are examples of 'accusatorial accustomed' judges adapting uncomfortably in an inquisitorial context: see Chapter Six.

Pre-panel preparation

Before the panel sat, the members would have had the opportunity to study the dossier, which formed the core of the evidence. Panel members told us that they spent considerable amounts of time reading the dossier:

> Some of them leap out at you as being really obvious, and then I think, 'Oh this is a pain going through the evidence to back this up' and some can take ages. I'll have read the file through quite a bit before I get here, by which I mean by the end of the week. And that may take an hour. And then the night before I'll go through it again taking notes, underlining, writing down areas of questions, and that – again depending on the file – might take half an hour or it might take over an hour (psychiatrist).

> I would start by asking myself the sorts of questions I would be asking if I were interviewing him, that's the first thing, so I'm looking for whatever it is, what the unanswered questions are and what I want to ask. I would also start to form a view in the same way that I would for a determinate or for a mandatory lifer, by looking at other people's views, the other reports and so on and try to get some consistent view as to whether the prisoner is and you know what the risk may or may not be and so on. So yes, I do form a view. I would think I am 75 per cent towards a decision before going into the [hearing] (independent).

> My dossiers come to the office, and I'm really curious, because I like to know who is it – and I read a couple of pages of the story. But when I'm ready to prepare I set aside time, and it depends on the size of the dossier... Each one of us has our own method of preparing for a case and I have my method, and I sort of write things down. I sometimes write a life history, a chronology, and sort of work out, from the day he was born and then charting events to give me a feeling of how things happened in his life, and that gives a picture of his life, and that takes time. I allow two foolscap pages for that (independent).

The DLP hearing

The hearing took place in a room set aside for the purpose, normally in the establishment's board room or in the chapel area. This quasi-formal occasion (more on this later) provided the panel's opportunity to hear and test evidence about the prisoner's level of risk and his or her progress in prison, normally in the presence of the prisoner[34]. The hearings normally lasted for more than an hour and consisted of questions from the panel (and often from a legal representative; less often from the Secretary of State's representative) to the prisoner, his or her witnesses and a representative from the prison. The typical DLP hearing could be divided into four stages (some of which overlap, but we have tried to address them separately), which we will consider in detail below:

- the pre-hearing discussion
- the hearing
- the deliberation
- drafting the reasons for the decision.

The pre-hearing discussion

At most hearings, the panel was circulated with one or more late papers (such as a psychiatrist's report, a home probation officer's report, an agreement from a probation hostel to accommodation, or a course assessment). This often included the Secretary of State's view, which was circulated at the hearing or shortly before it in 16 out of 52 cases (and at the wrong one[35], in one case). All late material had to be read and reflected on before the panel hearing started.

The pre-panel discussion was also a time for the panel members to explore what the key issues were. They sometimes agreed the key concerns (for example, risk factors such as substance/alcohol abuse; hostel arrangements; relationships; lack of insight or coping skills) which they intended to pursue during questioning. They also sometimes agreed who would ask which questions of witnesses. The psychiatrist was often delegated the responsibility of asking about issues relating to mental disorder.

They sometimes discussed the nature of the offence. During the pre-hearing discussion, provisional views were often exchanged about the likely outcome. Exchanges were made about the sort of case this seemed to be and the chances of favourable decisions being made. What the panel members seemed to do at this stage was establish the degree of consensus and where necessary, they began the process of gentle negotiation. An exchange might take place as follows:

---

34. Some prisoners dislike or become disillusioned with the process. Two chose not to attend and one or two were reluctant but were persuaded by non-panel members to attend.

35. We witnessed one case where the legal representative had been sent the wrong Secretary of State's view: when the Secretary of State's representative read out the view, which was different to the one that had been sent to the prisoner and to his representative, the solicitor was incensed, particularly since the Secretary of State's view also went against the conclusions of the Prison Service report writers.

Independent: There's a clear issue on this one, judge.

Judge: Yes indeed. His tariff is six, and he's done 11..... I am always worried by discretionary sentences. I feel it means the psychiatrist didn't know what lies behind [the offence]. There is a clear and simple issue – whether he stays at Category C, perhaps a more relaxed one, or should be tested in open conditions. The psychiatrist's report is quite positive and helpful to him. Views are a bit divided. Some say if he goes too soon, he might blow it. I'm not totally convinced.

Psychiatrist: This issue of a more relaxed regime gets a bit tricky – we can't compare prisons..

Judge: We could say he needs some further testing, knowing that it would lead to that outcome.

Psychiatrist: I am struggling to make the link between the work he has done and the offence. The trouble is, he is not going to be tested in the right way. He is clearly motivated, and has done some specific work too. We will have to listen to what everyone has to say. I have some concerns. I don't know what to make of his propensity to get depressed.

Judge: I am a bit concerned about his capacity to manage relationships.

Psychiatrist: He's in a bit of a catch 22.

Judge to psychiatrist: What do you think about the sexuality aspect?

Psychiatrist: It is normal to experiment – he has consistently denied more than that.

Judge: He seems intelligent. Above the run of many.

Independent: I want to ask about his education; his plans to go to university. The lifer governor thinks these are unrealistic.

Judge: There is not much to go on re his release plans.

All retained a more or less open mind at this stage. Having read the papers, and after relatively little detailed discussion, they agreed that they were ready, and asked the panel secretary to invite the participants in. They all entered, under the instruction of the panel secretary, and sat at the table, the prisoner facing the judge, the legal representative usually to the prisoner's left, and the Secretary of State's representative to the prisoner's right. The judge had the psychiatrist member on one side, and the independent on the other. The panel secretary sat at the end of the table, taking notes.

The hearing

The judge opened proceedings, normally by introducing himself and others in the room, and with reassuring words to the prisoner. The order in which witnesses were called, and the manner of questioning varied from panel to panel. Most judges discussed the order at the beginning of the hearing, and allowed the legal representative to help shape the order, but this did not always happen. Most frequently, the prisoner was called as the first witness, but other orders were not infrequent.

When the order was unusual, or was not the order requested by the legal representative, the legal representatives were sometimes put off their stride. For example, it was usual to hear the prisoner's witnesses first. This usually meant that where two psychologists were called, the independent psychologist, called on behalf of the prisoner, would be questioned first. The one to be called second may have had the advantage as they were able to refute the evidence of the other. For this reason, the prisoner's representative sometimes sought to call their independent psychologist after the Prison Service psychologist had been heard.

> [T]here is an expectation of a particular kind of procedure, which is reasonably good, I think, and suits the style of the hearing. So that you have a format of the Home Office introducing their case, the prisoner's representative introducing his or her case, the evidence being called in a logical order, the client goes first, usually that's the logical bit, I ask questions, the Home Office ask questions, you work methodically through, and then there's the closing statement. Some chairmen just dive in the middle. They will start asking questions, they will call witnesses before you've made an opening statement (legal representative).

The process could be disrupted when the chairman did not set a clear procedure or when the procedure agreed at the beginning was not then followed. Sometimes, the panel seemed to get distracted down a new route during the hearing, which meant the pattern agreed was not followed. In one example, the prisoner's legal representative was seeking release from a Category C prison. The only listed witnesses were the prisoner and his home probation officer. The judge asked most of the questions, and at one point the lifer liaison officer interrupted from the back of the room to help clarify an issue. He was then invited to come forward and become another witness. The legal representative lost control of the questioning and handed over the role of asking questions to the panel. The Secretary of State's representative was also left out of the process, to the extent that the judge turned to him at one stage and said, 'Don't worry I haven't forgotten you are there'.

Witnesses were normally examined first by the person who had asked them to attend, then by the other party, and then by the panel. However, sometimes the panel was encouraged by the legal representative to lead the questioning. This could be a successful way of ensuring that the panel heard directly from the prisoner. At other times, the panel threw themselves into the questioning, interrupting the legal representative, who might then fail to develop their case in the way that they had planned. At one panel, the psychiatrist on the panel asked the judge to stop interrupting, and to allow the prisoner to tell the facts his way. These issues will be developed further in Chapter Five.

Disputed evidence

Only rarely did we see any controversy about the admissibility of evidence. The prisoner and his representative saw everything the panel saw. There were two exceptional events: in one case the Secretary of State's representative decided to hand to the panel a document which LRU had refused to give to the prisoner's solicitor on the grounds that it contained security information (i.e. the document named those who had told the prison authorities of the prisoner's alleged drug dealing). The panel had not ordered him to do so: it was clearly a spontaneous decision on the part of the Secretary of State's representative that the document should be handed to the prisoner's representative (who read it, and passed it to the panel. It was not seen by the prisoner during the hearing). The second example was where the Secretary of State's representative on a recall hearing made references to matters which were not in the dossier[36].

In establishing and interpreting the evidence, the panel was not constrained by the traditional rules of evidence, for instance, the hearsay rule[37]. Both sides, and the panel, would freely ask a witness about events they have not witnessed. For example, in one case there had been a confrontation between the prisoner and an officer on the wing. The officer in question was not called as a witness, yet the officer who was called, who was not present at the incident, was asked to clarify the event in some detail. This 'hearsay' evidence causes deep resentment, particularly on the part of legal representatives, one of whom accused the Prison Service of 'incredible arrogance: a deep expectation that everyone is going to take as gospel whatever is said, irrespective of it being firmly founded'.

Some basic facts remained unclear even at the end of the hearing. One prisoner appeared to have been re-categorised (from D to C), but neither he nor his solicitor seemed to think this was the case. As the judge pointed out, 'if he's D, he should be in open conditions. If he's C, he should be told about it'. Another prisoner had been returned to closed conditions

---

36. Clearly the Prison Service knows much more about a prisoner than that which is in the DLP dossier. This was the only example we noticed of a clear hint at extraneous matters. We were surprised that the solicitor did not take issue with this.

37. The Civil Evidence Act 1995 s1(2) defines hearsay as 'a statement made otherwise than by a person while giving oral evidence in the proceedings which is tendered as evidence of the matters stated'. The evidential rule against hearsay means that witnesses can normally only give evidence of facts of which he or she has personal knowledge, but the rule is hedged around with complex exceptions: see for example Cross and Tapper, 1999, Chapter XIII-XV.

from Category D, and the allegations which had resulted in this were not thoroughly challenged.

More often legal representatives would seek to challenge the interpretation of events, rather than the facts themselves. It is important to note that 18 prisoners' cases were deferred during the course of our research, five of them once the panel had already convened. Most of these deferrals were due to factors beyond the panel's control, often because the prisoner wished to complete a course. However, some were related to disputed evidence (or evidence which might have been disputed).

The formality of the process
The Parole Board Rules establish that the panel should seek to avoid formality in the proceedings. In some ways, the process was court-like, with legal representatives sometimes referring to the 'prosecution' and the 'defence'. In other ways, efforts were made to reduce formality by introductions (occasional use of first names), deviations from procedures, and a reasonably friendly manner adopted by many panel members. The procedure was highly formal in the sense that prisoners were anxious, often dressed very smartly, and they assumed this was a powerful body with the discretion to make very significant decisions about them.

We found it necessary to distinguish formality of style or manner from procedural formality. Procedural formality, which concerns the order of witnesses, and the order and manner of their questioning, was addressed above, and varied. In terms of formality of style, the tone of the hearing was set by the judge, who would introduce the prisoner (and his or her legal representative) to the others present at the hearing. Most judges appeared well aware of what a difficult and important event the panel hearing is for the prisoner, and they attempted to put prisoners at ease:

Judge: You relax and we'll start by doing the talking.

Others were less sensitive: when one prisoner objected to observers, the judge announced harshly that he would not rule against the presence of the observers but would leave it up to the observers themselves whether they should leave. This created a hostile and somewhat confrontational atmosphere in the hearing.

Whether the tone remained informal (relaxed) would of course be affected by the other members of the panel, and indeed by the other parties involved. Psychiatrists sometimes dug very deeply into issues which would be difficult for anyone to discuss in front of strangers (for example, sexual fantasies, masturbation, remorse and rejection). In more than one case, prisoners were reduced to tears by the experience of being asked and having to answer very difficult questions. In one case, the Secretary of State's representative entered into a detailed and somewhat personal argument with the prisoner, which added to the tension. In another case, a judge refused to adjourn the hearing when the prisoner needed to go to the toilet: he allowed the prisoner to leave but refused to stop the proceedings.

The process was tiring for all concerned. Occasionally there were three hearings in one day. In these cases, the panel appeared exhausted by the third and the prisoner had a less full hearing.

The advantages of an informality of style were that they would help relax all the participants and prisoners might feel more able to speak freely, ask questions and answer fully. Most panel members believed that the panel hearing should be fairly formal: it was a serious business for both the prisoner and for the public, not a social gathering. Too much formality or informality could handicap the process.

One or two participants were conscious that too much informality left them vulnerable:

> Remember I sit in a court, if there's any uproar or something I disagree with, I leave the court. Whereas in a parole board hearing, I'm in a room with some person...and if there's any fuss or whatever, I can't leave, I'm stuck with it. And occasionally prisoners do become abusive (judge).

> I had a small concern with x. I know she can be violent, and I thought 'mmm, what would happen if she decides to have a violent outburst? And then it will be me who gets it'. So, the only thing I might say about [informality] would be about having officers in attendance to control her, but that makes it a bit more formal. Or seating it differently, so that there isn't the proximity of closeness between me and her (lifer governor).

One prisoner felt that the process would improve if it was more informal: if for example the prisoner joined the panel for lunch and they met him in a more social setting.

Differences in decision-making

Hearings differed in significant ways. The most obvious differences in the decision-making process was whether or not the panel was being asked to direct release. The issues on a release case were often different to those at most hearings held in Category C or B establishments, where there was usually no question of release. Thus in a number of cases we observed at open prisons, the questions concerned the detail of the release plan. In a few cases, the judge told the prisoner during the hearing that he was, in effect, 'pushing at an open door' and that the panel was concerned only with decisions about licence conditions. The key issue, on the other hand, in a Category A prison was more likely to be whether there was anything specific that the panel could do to help 'move the prisoner on'.

As a process, panels were conducted remarkably consistently. Their manner differed, partly due to the role of the judge as chairman (see Chapter Five), but also for other reasons of style and personality of the other participants. Some panels performed better than others. There were three examples of the formal procedure being abandoned in favour of a much more informal procedure, and these departures (when radical) unsettled the prisoners and their legal representatives. Levels of involvement by panel members differed, but we did not see any member excluded. They were all able to participate if they had something specific to ask. One panel member complained that he felt 'superfluous'. But this was largely due to the lack of any psychiatric component to the hearing (this question of whether specialist members attend only in their capacity as a specialist is an interesting question, which we reflect upon a little in Chapter Five). We witnessed one independent member and one psychiatrist admonish the chair when he was being unduly fierce, or too lax. Despite some important differences in the types of cases observed (for example, HMPs were regarded with a little less caution and more 'helpfulness' than lifers sentenced whilst adult), we felt the panels were very consistent. The questions the panel were addressing differed according to the type of case being heard, and the nature of the risk posed, but the process was similar throughout. Panels approached their task in a very similar, conscientious and serious way, conducting their task to the best of their ability, despite some views that panels held in high security prisons were 'not real panels'.

The deliberation

Once the other participants had left the room, the panel discussed the likely decision, having heard all the evidence. They deliberated, identifying issues that confirmed their provisional view, or sharing with their colleagues thoughts about revising their initial view. The judge normally started, but sometimes we witnessed the judge invite the other two panel members to 'go first'. This process was remarkably quick, after what were usually long hearings. This case, for example, was about whether to release a recalled prisoner or recommend a period in a resettlement prison first. The prisoner, his wife, his home probation officer and legal representative had all argued powerfully for release [from observation notes]:

Judge: Thank you very much. [He explains that they will hear in the next seven days – the prisoner and wife both know the way it's going. They all leave.]

Judge: I don't want to sound arrogant but I'm pretty clear in my mind that he should go to [a specific resettlement prison].
Psychiatrist: [The home probation officer] came round to our view. She agreed that he should be treated sequentially; that's not how she started; her evidence – her report and her oral evidence contradict each other. I think all the evidence is one way. From the pattern, there is a risk. There are so many issues unresolved. The whole scene is rather horrendous. The dynamics of their relationship are quite incendiary.
Independent: I am 100 per cent behind it [the specific resettlement prison].
Judge: Thank you very much. That's sewn up then. Let's have lunch. [4 minutes!].

Table 4.1 shows the amount of time panels spent hearing evidence, making their decision and in formulating their reasons. It has already been noted how little time panels spend formally discussing the key decisions they have to make, since the decision itself is really the culmination of the process.

Table 4.1: Length of DLP hearings*

	All cases	Recalls	DLPs and HMPs
Range of length of hearings	8 minutes – 4 hours (average = 1 hour 19 minutes)	1 hour 5 minutes – 4 hours (average = 2 hours 35 minutes)	8 minutes – 3 hours 16 minutes (average = 56 minutes)
Range of length of deliberations	0 – 20 minutes (average = 5 minutes 50 seconds)	1 – 10 minutes (average = 4 minutes 30 seconds)	0 – 20 minutes (average = 6 minutes)
Range of time drafting reasons	0 – 50 minutes (average = 30 minutes)	20 – 40 minutes (average = 32 minutes 30 seconds)	0 – 50 minutes (average = 27 minutes)

(* approximate calculations based on cases where information was recorded)

The panel may continue to test the evidence at this stage, discussing it in detail with each other:

What did you make of [a witness]...?
I thought Ms X stood up well to the questions, didn't you? etc.

The panel would at this stage simplify the evidence, and make assumptions arising from it:

I never believe what people say about their alcohol consumption.

She seems a bit of a victim (about a wife who had withdrawn her allegation against her husband).

That's the sort of woman who strikes up a relationship with a lifer.

His failure to turn up at probation appointments backs up the evidence of him being a drinker.

But he did break his wife's nose [this had been a disputed allegation at an earlier hearing, which was never resolved].

We saw consensus far more often than we saw negotiation:

Psychiatrist: What a bummer. We need to find a clever way to phrase all that in the direction we want; that's all we can do. He's not asking for release or open. It all depends on whether there is a place available for him. We need to try. He's not going anywhere without [our recommendation for a SOTP course].
Judge: It was realistic not to push the boundaries too much.

And:

Judge: He is still a danger to the public. He should go to B or C. I simply can't see a move straight to open.
Psychiatrist: It's absurd what the solicitor is asking for.
Judge: He must have some homosexual tendency, am I wrong?
Psychiatrist: You are right, he may not be completely, he may not be a paedophile. But he is not a well adjusted heterosexual.
Judge: I don't see that there's a case for an early review either. He needs to go to a less secure place and do the booster.

In another case, there were (as there often were) severe constraints on the panel as to the decision they could make. But we were still surprised by how briefly 'the decision' was made and how little discussion there was about the nature of the risks posed:

> The legal representative sums up. 12.35 p.m.: It is a question of where the work should be done. The issue of [a specific special hospital] should be explored further.
>
> Judge: Is it necessarily [this secure hospital?].
>
> Legal representative: No, of course. There is the issue of transfer to hospital, in a secure setting. She is 'sincerely curious' about that option. A poor prognosis can be improved. She knows the limits. It may be the most effective place for her to be treated. She could, however, use the remaining time in prison constructively. We are not asking for release, or transfer to open at this stage.
>
> 12.40: Judge: you will get a letter in the next seven days. For the next five minutes, please remain outside the room, just in case we need to ask you back in.
>
> All, except for the panel and panel secretary, leave.
>
> Heavy sighs. Judge: My view is she is highly dangerous at present – she should have another review in two years. We can see if we can write into the letter some oblique suggestions to get the Home Office to think about her case. We do seem to have a window of opportunity here [where she seems willing to co-operate with treatment].
>
> Drafting…What she has done in the prison system…the possibility should be explored for transfer… ETS may be an important first step. Group work is a challenge she needs to face up to. She should be assessed for the newly established ETS course. [Straight into drafting; no discussion of decision.]
>
> Judge: Thank you. I'll write something down and I'll show it to you after I've written it. We don't want them back, do we? Tell them they are not required.

So the deliberation was often very brief (although refinements of it continued into the drafting stage), unless there were serious differences of opinion to begin with:

> Judge: Well, there's been a full ventilation. Anything else you want to explore or shall we send them away? Do we accept the Secretary of State's view or do we think that the time has come for him to have another chance? I have a view, but after you…
>
> Psychiatrist: I think he is ready. The drug support he is getting here is available elsewhere. There's been no risk of violence for a long time.
>
> Independent: It is difficult. I think there's a high chance that he'll fail. But he won't fail for violence and he needs two years in open.
>
> Judge: I take the other view on this chap. OK the offence was not drug related but drugs is now a deep-seated problem. It is a serious on-going temptation and I think

he's going to fail in the community and so we should go on a slowly slowly basis but to give him a better chance of success. He's pressed the self-destruct button – which doesn't augur well. I think he should remain in Cat C and should be reviewed in 12 months time.

[At this stage it feels as though it's 2 against 1, the judge being in the minority.]

Independent: He's done 35 sessions of R&R.

Judge: Yes, but they want to see how he implements it. Also we need to get the message across to him. He's got to crack the drug problem.

Psychiatrist: I still feel the pressure on him is worse here than elsewhere.

Independent: He started his criminal career at 11. My doubt is that he never mentioned his victims.

Psychiatrist: He is vulnerable. If we keep him here, he must have an early review

[the psychiatrist is moving towards the judge's position].

Judge to independent: It is a majority decision: would you be happy to keep him in Cat C and ask for further information?

[The judge seems impatient to be finished and persuades his colleagues to take the cautious route.]

Where there was discussion, it was clear that the composition of the panel often facilitated a careful consideration of the case:

> You try to be as objective as you can and having three members gives you the opportunity to do that. It does require each of the members to play their full part in arguing their particular corner (independent member).

Partly because of the nature of the cases, there was often considerable consensus. The facts were established during the hearing and all panel members tended to operate with the very clear emphasis on public protection. There were times when we observed consensus amongst panel members, where we might have felt as observers that the evidence was insufficient or the prisoner had become over-labelled and stuck in a negative spiral in their current establishment. Panel members were infrequently critical of 'the case against' transfer and release. 'The case for' was often dependent on the legal representative – and as we discuss in a later section, they were of variable experience, quality and ambition for the prisoner. Sometimes disagreement did happen, however, and one panel member would challenge assumptions being made by the others, and change the nature of the decision being made:

Interviewer: How confident do you feel about the decisions you reach?

Judge: I feel comfortable with them. I know that wasn't the word you used. Yes I feel reasonably confident about the decisions I reach. Occasionally I have difficulties with my other members, who want to do something that I don't want to do, and I don't feel very confident about that. It's based on majority viewpoint.

Some panel members argued that the decisions more often started off split on DLP cases, because of the complexities of the cases.

Drafting the reasons for the decision

Even at this stage the panel was sometimes testing the evidence. Panel members would continue to comment that the reasons did not seem very strong, and would go back to mention other evidence which might have influenced them. They would work out their views as they drafted. This is a case from one of our early observations. Here we were again surprised by how little time was devoted to the question of risk during the formal deliberation, although it emerged throughout the later stages of the drafting:

Judge: I am very pleased that the solicitor has taken a realistic approach – she has persuaded him on our behalf, that he shouldn't be looking for release.

Psychiatrist: We shouldn't make a recommendation to [a specific prison], but we can make a recommendation for 'one-to-one' treatment. [They discuss SOTP for the educationally challenged. He needs that on a 'one-to-one' basis.]

[All three chat equally – all making their own contributions to the discussion. An evenly balanced panel – all looking for an answer at this stage. Not addressing the question of risk at all.] [38]

Judge: The question of treatment is their problem... Now let's see how we can phrase this. We are not directing for release, or open... What did we take account of? We want him to focus on the one-to-one work just undertaken... He has done no offending behaviour work up to now. He realistically didn't ask for release. He remains a high risk – that is what is being said, it is what the sentencing judge said, and he has not moved from that. We don't want to raise his hopes – we must phrase accordingly. [The judge is doing the drafting – assisted by the panel secretary. He dictates ... 'we took into consideration the fact that two fires recently started in your cell' (assumption of guilt).]

---

38. Comments in square brackets are notes made during the observations by the researchers.

Independent: What about, 'the panel is pleased to notice that in one-to-one sessions particularly with officer x, some change in attitude has taken place, in that you acknowledge that you need to work on your offending behaviour...'

The panel secretary prods: He doesn't really say that, no, but his solicitor does. He still seems to be interested in fires. It is still a main interest.

Judge:... 'much work still needs to be done and by reason of your learning difficulties'...are we going to get in trouble with the Prison Service if we say one-to-one? ...

Psychiatrist: Only if it is not available...

Judge:... it would be best to do this on a one-to-one basis, preferably by an experienced psychologist (or caseworker...) –

Panel secretary: – do you want to expand on 'much work'?

Judge: No thank you.

Psychiatrist: We want a detailed report at the next review for the parole board by a doctor or specialist in forensic learning difficulties, ...or a forensic consultant in mental handicap.. To advise on the best method of treatment, whether in or out of prison.

[Spent 15 minutes so far on their discussion of the draft – rather than on discussion of their decision....They seem to be wanting to 'manage his case' rather than 'assess his risk'.]

Judge:...We don't want to give him the impression that he is close to release, because he is a long way from that..

Psychiatrist: If you deny the offence, we can't hold people back for that...

Judge: We are assessing risk, he was a high risk, he has done no work, and so he is still a high risk. 'Risk, risk, risk, is our duty'.... 'Our considered view is that you remain a high risk. This is not likely to take less than two years and therefore the panel does not recommend an early review.'

Judge to panel secretary: You and I can refine that on the train.

The panel's written decision was a hybrid document, with many functions. It had to explain the decision on risk, but it also had other purposes:

Say nothing about Category C. That's internal. We'll really get up their noses if we do that...

I don't think we should specify which prison, but we could say one-to-one work...

If they get enough recommendations for cognitive skills one-to-one, it might help their funding requests...

Remember this solicitor has a hotline to the Divisional Court...

Let's keep it brief... I don't want to write a book...I don't want to go into too much detail...

The judicial review will happen on the front page of the local paper.

I'll agree to 'open' with a slightly heavy heart as I can see the News of the World headline in five years' time.

We must mention the Home Secretary's support so he gets the blame too if anything goes wrong.

The panel secretary could provide the panel with a model, if they requested it.

Proforma/Model Letter

1. The Crime Sentences Act 1997 requires the Parole Board to direct your release only if it is satisfied that it is no longer necessary for the protection of the public that you be confined. The panel of the Board who considered your case on... was (not) so satisfied and has therefore (not) directed your release (at this stage). (This decision is binding upon the Secretary of State.)

2. The panel considered all the documents before them, including your written representations, together with the statements made by you,.... and the submissions made by your legal representative,.... at the hearing.

3. (a). In reaching its decision the panel took particular account of .... and concluded that you remain a risk because (unless or until).......

    (b) In reaching its decision that you no longer need to be confined, the panel took account.........

4. (a) The panel recommended to the Secretary of State that you should be considered for transfer to Category _ prison [and that your case should be reviewed in.....]. It made this (these) recommendations because......

4. (b). The panel made no recommendation to the Secretary of State with regard to transfer [or early review] [but recommended that your case should be reviewed

in ......]. [The panel would expect an up-to-date psychiatric report to be provided for the next review].

4.   (c) In directing your release the panel recommended that your life licence should include the standard conditions of a life licence together with the following extra condition (s):

5.   The panel was concerned that.......

6.   The panel noted the progress which you made in ... and (but) hoped that.........

6.1. The decision not to release you is binding upon the Secretary of State, although it is a matter for him to decide whether to accept the recommendation that you.....

7.   Copies of this letter are being sent to the Governor, the Prison Service and your legal representative.

Panel Chairman[39]

In practice, however, the panel secretary was not often asked for the proforma. The judge had normally brought his or her own, in some cases with a draft already written (or in two cases a draft of two possible outcomes). There was no hint that this extent of preparation pre-empted decision-making: indeed, the judge made it clear on several occasions that he or she had come with alternative versions. Normally the judge took the lead in drafting, with varying input from others. The letters were drafted with great care, though panels varied enormously in the involvement of the various members in the process. Practice seemed to depend on make-up of the panel, and on the individuals concerned. Some psychiatrists, perhaps particularly those who were involved in Mental Health Review Tribunals, took a very active or equal role, others took less of a role, or (in a small number of cases) a minimal one. It was not unusual for the two non-chairing members to talk to each other about other matters whilst the judge drafted. On other occasions, the independent member was clearly a skilled drafter and would get very involved. This drafting process also depended on the experience of the judge: the less experienced needed more help. Team drafting was not easy and we witnessed some problems with dictation:

Judge: Hang on. Your brain is 100 yards ahead of mine. Say it more slowly.

Sometimes there was a definite team effort (normally of two rather than three):

Judge: Who else will scribble?
Psychiatrist: OK (both write for a short time).

39. In fact the decision letters were sent out in the name of the Chief Executive of the Parole Board, signed by one of the secretariat staff.

Judge: How are you doing, friend?
Psychiatrist: Not very well (reads his out).
Judge: That's lovely.

The length of the reasons varied greatly. One judge said, 'If I'm not releasing, I think we have to put in lots of reasons; if we are releasing, we should say less'.

Sometimes an issue the prisoner raised which he thought would have been positive was used to justify a negative decision. One prisoner, an arsonist with a low IQ, had recently started one-to-one counselling work, and this was mentioned in the reasons as a justification for not moving him on (that is, the fact he had started to co-operate was interpreted as a reason for holding him back).

The role of the panel secretary at this stage of the process was varied: some would be listening carefully and would interrupt and offer advice, others would be outside preparing lunch/tea. At the end of the drafting process, the judge would read back the draft to his colleagues. At this point some panel secretaries also added comments; others said nothing.

Occasionally there was some disagreement:

Case 1
Independent: Should we give an alternative: should we say that if the Secretary of State does not accept our view, should we recommend a 12 month review?
Psychiatrist: No he doesn't oppose Cat D.
Judge: Oh no, we needn't give the Secretary of State an alternative.

Case 2
Psychiatrist: Mention the tariff date.
Independent: We don't usually.

The decision letters were not simply a letter to the prisoner saying why he or she could or could not be released or moved to open. It could be used to push forward a 'stuck' prisoner:

The panel noted and understood your desire to have a structured plan for your progress through the prison system and recommended that serious consideration be given to your transfer to a Category C prison and to appropriate courses to be carried out there and further that if you are so transferred to Category C prison your next review should take place one year after your transfer, as the panel felt this period would be sufficient for the required work to be completed (letter).

As some panel members said, 'we specify which areas need to be addressed, but not the availability of the courses'. The letter can be used to relay a message from a prisoner to the Prison Service:

> The panel noted the fact that you expressed your wish to be transferred to HMP xxx so that you could be closer to your family. The panel hoped that you understood that recommendations as to transfer between secure prisons does not fall within their remit... (letter).

It can be used to criticise the Home Secretary:

> The panel considered the Secretary of State's recommendation of a further period in a resettlement unit but was convinced that the benefits of such a placement would be far outweighed in this particular case by the availability of home and the support of your mother and stepfather in the locality where you wish to get employment and where you will be supervised by your probation officer of long standing. The panel also noted the success of eight home leave visits and that not one of the reports was in favour of a resettlement unit (letter).

Panels were sometimes concerned to avoid blame, or to share blame, perhaps to avoid criticisms if anything went wrong:

> Psychiatrist: [in a case where the panel directed release:] ...Mention that the Home Secretary supports release.
> Judge: Yes, I've stuck him at the top.

Or:

> Panel secretary: Mention that the home probation officer said he was ready for open.

Letters followed a standard pattern; what one judge called, 'the usual terrible old claptrap'. Other participants, particularly legal representatives, would welcome more detail in the letter:

> That's the only evidence we ever get about the decision-making process, once we left the room, and one often wonders what goes on (legal representative).

I have a problem sometimes where they are telling the Secretary of State something; say for example, they are making a recommendation about a certain treatment, and they are basing it upon evidence that they have had during the hearing. They are very often very lazy and they simply don't set out what it is that they have taken account of during the course of the hearing on which they are basing their decision. And what they forget is that the Secretary of State wasn't there. Nobody from the Home Office Prison Service was there. The person who was there was some LLO who's not going to report back anything. And so they completely fail to do the most important part of their task, because if they are trying to persuade the Secretary of State to do something they have got to tell him the basis for doing it, so that he has to justify the basis for refusing to do it, by reference to what they've said. So reasoning can be very poor and ill thought out. They don't think about why it is they're saying so and similarly, when they are making their decisions, quite often they don't cogently explain them (legal representative).

These latter stages of the process – the deliberation and the drafting of the letter – were sometimes rushed and seemed to be carried out less carefully than the hearing stage of the procedure (see Table 4.1).

Licence conditions

All lifers who are released from prison are released on a licence, which remains in force for the rest of the individual's life. The licence contains six standard conditions:

1.   He/She shall place him/herself under the supervision of whichever probation officer is nominated for this purpose from time to time.

2.   He/She shall on release report to the probation officer so nominated, and shall keep in touch with that officer in accordance with that officer's instructions.

3.   He/She shall, if his/her probation officer so requires, receive visits from that officer where the licence holder is living.

4.   He/She shall reside only where approved by his/her probation officer.

5.   He/She shall work only where approved by his/her probation officer and shall inform his/her probation officer at once if he/she loses his/her job.

6. He/she shall not travel outside Great Britain without the prior permission of his/her probation officer.

In most cases where the panel was discussing release, they simply imposed the standard licence conditions. Occasionally others were discussed or added. The most common were residence requirements, treatment requirements, or (more rarely) a requirement that the licencee avoid a certain geographical area.

Geographical restrictions were imposed to protect victims (or as one judge put it, 'to assuage the victim lobby'), but panels were reluctant to impose them partly because they were difficult to enforce in practice and partly because they might put unreasonable limitations on the prisoner's freedom (e.g. their ability to take a train through the proscribed area).

Other possible conditions were sometimes discussed, but were normally rejected:

Judge: Can we make a curfew as part of the licence?
Independent: No.
Psychiatrist: And we certainly can't make it a condition of the licence that he's in employment!

Once the judge had finished his draft, he invariably read it back to his colleagues who at that stage would sometimes add a final detail:

You might like to mention his attitude to alcohol.

Have we said enough about risk?

Mention the tariff date.

The letters were completed whilst the panel was still together, though on one occasion it was agreed that since the panel hearing had taken longer than expected the judge could put together a draft on his own which he would then show to his colleagues when they reconvened the next morning for another case. The judge sometimes tidied up the draft with the panel secretary, for example on the train afterwards, or the Parole Board secretariat would sometimes make minor amendments in the office in the next few days, but our comparisons of our notes with the letters actually sent to prisoners revealed no significant changes.

As far as we know, all prisoners received the decision within seven or eight days. Some learned at the hearing: two of those who were being recommended for open were told so at their hearing in Category C; two of the released were told they were pushing at an open door and that the panel was only interested in licence conditions. Several interviewees suggested that prisoners should be told at the hearing itself. The waiting process was certainly painful:

> After they'd gone, I was looking out the window and I saw these people walking out of the gate and I said to myself they already know their decision, they already knew the decision that they were going to make, they already knew what they wanted to do and yet they were leaving me for a week to stew and I thought to myself, why? Why are you doing this? Why do I have to sit there for another week going absolutely crazy. It was horrible, it was really, really horrible. In fact worse than actually waiting for the actual DLP to start. ... Maybe not actually telling you there and then but maybe a day or two afterwards, but a week. Seven days. It's just torment (prisoner).

However, most people felt that a 'cooling off period' was appropriate, especially in the case of a 'knock back'.

Strengths and limitations of the DLP decision-making process

The greatest strength of the DLP process was the oral hearing. Prisoners felt that their cases were being taking seriously and the panel had the opportunity to explore issues raised in the dossier more thoroughly than was possible with paper hearings. This is not to say that the process was necessarily 'better' than a paper hearing in terms of outcome: this is an area in which hard measures of success are hard to come by. The measures of success used were largely negative: many participants quoted a recall rate of 31 per cent, which was seen as a measure of failure. It was not clear that 'preventative' recalls were rightly seen as failures, yet this was the measure of 'failure' most often mentioned. It surprised us that we were not often offered the number of released discretionary lifers who had been convicted of serious offences. Other measures of success/failure might have included statistics on non-violation of licence conditions (see Burgess, 1928).

A subtle advantage of having the prisoner present was that prisoners believed that the system was fairer. The oral hearing was empowering. It allowed the prisoner to have a say, and to listen. However, not all prisoners welcomed it: some found it intrusive and frustrating.

It was difficult to know the impact of the prisoner's presence on the decision: for example, the number of prisoners who were not released because their presence confirmed or aggravated panel members' concerns. The oral hearing also allowed the panel to question report writers face to face. It was a very thorough mode of inquiry, involving a wide variety of expertise. As a forum, there may be no better way of assessing risk than the current panel hearing.

The other participants benefited from the oral hearing too:

> ... just to get other people's point of view... we were able to pick out one particular issue which I found useful and I wouldn't have thought about clearly on my own. It can be quite an isolating experience supervising a lifer ... It was a chance to weigh up my report and measure it a bit (home probation officer).

The process was clearly limited by the quality and timeliness of the dossiers. The two major problems were the time lag between the preparation of the report and the hearing (which militates against panels ordering early reviews), and the lateness of reports. There were also concerns about the nature and quality of dossier reports. Whilst dossiers were thorough, consideration should be given to whether they could be simplified. The collection of information for the dossier is not simply an exercise in collecting relevant material. The dossier was 'constructed' from various sources, and one fact can become more significant simply by being repeated[40]. There should be some sort of quality check on dossiers, including feedback from the Parole Board to the Prison Service about what material is most useful.

Decisions and outcomes

We turn now to look at the decisions that panels reached, and the eventual outcomes of these decisions.

---

40. See McConville, Saunders and Leng (1991).

Figure 4.1: Decisions made at observed hearings

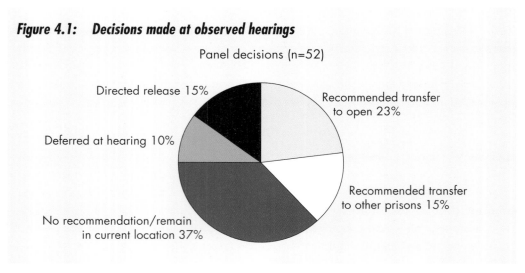

Panel decisions (n=52)

Directed release 15%

Recommended transfer to open 23%

Deferred at hearing 10%

Recommended transfer to other prisons 15%

No recommendation/remain in current location 37%

Recall decisions

In all five cases where the panel was considering representations against recall at the first oral hearing since the prisoner's return to prison, the recall was confirmed. The role of the panel at this stage was not simply to confirm recall, but also to make a fresh assessment on the necessity of detention and whether this detention should be in open conditions. This was not always done.

Release decisions

At the time of writing, eight of the prisoners whose cases we had observed, and a further prisoner who had objected to his panel being observed, had been released. All the prisoners whose release was directed were released within 36 days of the DLP hearing (the average was 19 days with a range from 10 to 36 days), or within 29 days of receiving the decision letter. All of those whose release was directed were located in open conditions at the time of the DLP, and in terms of status, three were HMPs, five were DLPs and one was a recalled prisoner on his third review post-recall. Two of the prisoners were released after their first oral hearing. The average time served of those released was 14 years and 7 months (ranging from 8 years 4 months to 21 years) and they had served an average of 4 years 10 months beyond tariff (with a range from 0 to 14 years). In terms of index offences, one had been convicted of wounding with intent to cause actual bodily harm, three had been convicted of rape and two had been convicted of manslaughter. All those released had been legally represented and in every case witnesses had been called (a psychologist in four cases and a home probation officer in all cases but one).

Of those prisoners whose release was directed, the Secretary of State's view in three cases had been that the prisoner presented an acceptable risk and had suggested licence conditions. In another four cases the Secretary of State's view had been that they were not suitable for release, but the panel had decided against the Secretary of State's view. In two further cases the Secretary of State had not been 'in a position to provide a view on suitability for release'.

Only on one occasion did we witness a full panel hearing at an open prison at which the panel made the decision not to release. In this case both the prison probation officer and the home probation officer were witnesses at the hearing and all the reports were in support of release to a hostel. However, the Secretary of State had stated that he was 'not in a position to provide a view on suitability for release due to the continued uncertainty regarding the release plan'. (It had not been possible to locate accommodation in a safe and secure environment to meet the prisoner's needs and to provide adequate protection for the public on a long-term basis.) The panel recommended a further review in 12 months and stated in the decision letter that this 'would allow time for those responsible for the preparation of a release plan to find out whether a specialist housing association or charity could provide accommodation and intensive support, which would provide adequate protection for the public'. We observed three DLPs in open conditions which began but were deferred, one because the home probation officer and psychologist were not present; one due to lack of up-to-date reports by the home probation officer, psychologist or psychiatrist; and the third because the prisoner was pending the outcome of a Governor's adjudication. At the subsequent deferred hearing, the panel decided to release this third prisoner.

What did the released prisoners have in common? In terms of reports, one common feature was that in every case the home probation officer had recommended release. In all seven of the release cases where a psychiatrist had made recommendations, their reports had supported release on licence. A prison psychologist had recommended release in five of the release cases, the lifer liaison officer had recommended release in eight of the cases, and the personal officers and prison probation officers had recommended release in six cases each. In three of the release cases all the reports recommended release. In fact in seven of the nine release cases, the panel's decision to release accorded with the majority of the reports. However, in one case there was only one report writer in favour of release (the home probation officer). The Secretary of State's view was that that prisoner was unsuitable for release.

Some prisoners sought release from closed conditions, all unsuccessfully. Three of the prisoners who were recommended for transfer to open conditions had been seeking a direction for release.

Recommendations for open conditions

No prisoner in our study was released unless he was in open conditions[41]. Therefore, a key hurdle for a lifer was to reach open conditions. Panels may only recommend this, and the Secretary of State decides whether or not to accept the recommendation. He controlled the decision. Of the 12 prisoners whom the panel recommended for transfer to open conditions, at the time of writing, two prisoners had actually been transferred and in five further cases the Secretary of State had agreed to the move, but they had not yet been transferred. The other cases were still under consideration by the Secretary of State.

Did the cases recommended for transfer to open conditions share any common characteristics? In all but two cases the prisoner had been located in a Category C prison at the time of the DLP (one was in a Category B prison and the other was a recalled prisoner in a local prison). In half of the 12 cases, the Secretary of State's view had been that the prisoner should not be moved to open conditions. In another four cases he had had no view. Thus in only two cases where transfer to open was recommended by the panel had the Secretary of State supported this move. In the two cases where the Home Secretary had recommended transfer to open neither prisoner had moved at the time of writing (December 1999). Their panels had taken place in September and October. In two of the four cases where the Secretary of State had expressed no view, but where the panel had recommended transfer to open, the prisoners had moved to open conditions.

There was no discernible pattern in the cases in which the panels recommended transfer to open conditions in terms of which report writers' recommendations were followed. In three of the 12 cases the majority of reports had not recommended open and in these three cases the Secretary of State's view had been against transfer to open. In four cases where transfer to open had been recommended, it had been the prisoner's first oral hearing. In each case the prisoner had had legal representation, but in three of these cases there had been no witnesses.

In total 12 prisoners had sought a recommendation for transfer to open conditions (some of those who were recommended for transfer to open had asked for release). Of these only two were unsuccessful, and in both cases the Secretary of State had not supported transfer to an open prison. In both cases the panel had felt that more work on sexual offending was required, despite the fact that in one case the prisoner had been in open conditions for two years but had been transferred back to closed conditions in order to undertake the SOTP (which he did).

41. Release when not in open conditions may occur occasionally.

Other recommendations

Of the eight cases where the panel recommended transfer to another prison other than to open conditions, six were recommendations to transfer the prisoner from a Category B to a Category C prison (of which two were recommendations for transfer for purposes of specifically identified offending behaviour work), one was in support of transfer from one Category C prison to another, and one was in support of a transfer but without specifying to which category of prison[42]. All these recommendations built on suggestions which emerged either in the reports, or at the hearing. At the time of writing these recommendations had been accepted by the Secretary of State in three cases. One prisoner moved within a month of the recommendation, and another was transferred after three months. In one case a recalled prisoner was transferred from a local prison to a resettlement prison 16 days after the panel hearing (which was held some eight months after his recall). In three cases the prisoner was actually transferred to another Category B establishment (despite the recommendation by the panel of transfer to Category C) and three recommendations for transfers were simply rejected.

In 13 cases, panels had recommended an early review, the majority for 12 months' time (three for 18 months' time). We do not know whether these recommendations were accepted. In 12 cases the panel recommended further offending behaviour work in the form of specific accredited programmes and in seven cases they suggested further assessment.

Summary of decision outcomes

We have observed then a process that works well, but which may have little impact in practice. All recalls were confirmed. All nine prisoners who were released were in open conditions, and had the support of their probation officers. Future research might be able to explore whether those prisoners who were released were released earlier or later than they might otherwise have been if there had not been a DLP process. Only two of the decisions to release were 'surprising' in that a majority of report writers did not support release. In cases where panels made recommendations, it is difficult to assess the extent to which the Secretary of State's later decisions were affected by the panel's recommendation.

---

42. The panel's view was often worded in the decision letter in such a way as to encourage the Prison Service to take a particular action but without wording it too strongly. For example, 'the panel recommend that serious consideration be given to your transfer to a Category C prison', and 'the panel believes that consideration should be given by the Prison Service to assessing you for a move to a Category C prison'. Sometimes they added a reminder that the decision did not fall within the remit of the panel.

Issues arising from the DLP process

During our observations of the hearing, a number of themes emerged, which merit separate consideration, and which we consider below. These concerned the accuracy and timeliness of the DLP dossiers; delays and deferrals within the process; and the differences between (especially first oral) recall hearings and ordinary DLPs.

The quality and accuracy of DLP dossiers

'It is not too much to say…that the adequacy of parole decisions is dependent upon the adequacy of the documentation of cases submitted' (Report of the Parole Board 1968; in Bottomley, 1984: 28).

How far is the role played by documentation still crucial in 1999 when, in DLP cases, oral hearings now constitute the key decision-making forum? Panel members spent several hours reading dossiers in advance of a hearing and normally arrived at the establishment having come to a preliminary view, and certainly having highlighted areas of concern for exploration during the review. The dossiers provided a fairly full picture of the offender, his or her offence, background and behaviour in prison. They enabled panel members to form 'a cumulative picture' of the individual, their attitude to the offence and towards prison, and their resettlement plans.

Most of those panel members we interviewed felt confident that they came to a hearing well informed, but prepared to have their provisional view altered by the proceedings. Issues militating against release identified in dossiers were inevitably explored, often at length.

We examined the files of 52 prisoners during our study; and we included one or two questions on the helpfulness of the dossiers in our questionnaire. Interviewees, and those with whom we held informal discussions, criticised the quality and timeliness of dossiers throughout the research despite an assumption we found among our research sponsors that dossiers were in general of a satisfactory quality. We observed some of the usual limitations of any reliance upon record-based information, perhaps especially in prison.

Coker and Martin identified five overlapping concerns about the use of official documentation when making risk decisions in their study of parole decision-making (Coker and Martin, 1985: 47):

1. Reports tend to be subjective and judgemental rather than objective, and reflect staff perception of the interaction between themselves and the prisoner.

2. There are dangers that opinions are formed early in a prisoner's career and then subsequent information is used to support that view.

3. There are dangers that out-of-date material is re-used, and that negative labels may stick.

4. The material may be organised to suit standardised forms rather than an individual's case.

5. The prisoner does not see these reports and cannot correct inaccuracies.

The last of these objections has been largely addressed by open reporting, but the first four remained a concern. Unlike most official records used in research, DLP dossiers were compiled and used for a single purpose: they were intended to assist in the process of risk assessment. But like many official records, they could be contradictory, unreliable, selective and biased (Kitsuse and Cicourel, 1963; Liebling, 1992: 91-3). Files tended to present a grimmer picture of a prisoner than other sources based on contact, and they could not tell 'the whole story'. Valuable contextual information might be missing. Sometimes information contained in reports was attributed a significance it might not possess[43].

On the other hand, we found that DLP dossiers were by far the most comprehensive and carefully presented official records we had seen to date, with a useful summary of the case and each report writers' recommendations at the front of each file. Despite a certain amount of repetition, they were of a high standard.

---

43. Hawkins, 1983, uses the example of B's sex play with a six-year-old when he was a boy, which might be regarded in another setting as 'normal' behaviour, but in a prison record, especially the record of a rapist, it can be made to appear ominous. More striking, perhaps, is the fact that it was considered significant to record that B's mother had a traumatic incident at the age of seven when she was in a car accident and saw her mother decapitated. This displays not only the salience of history and the almost infinite capacity of pieces of supposedly 'relevant' data to survive in files, but also the kind of theorising which deems such material to be relevant. The decision-maker may be led into speculating that the traumatic incident may have affected the way in which B's mother later brought him up, which in turn had some (unspecified) link with his subsequent sexual misconduct. Or he may be able to deduce a different meaning from the information. At the very least it is likely that the board member will be led to believe that its very presence in the file must mean something (Hawkins, 1983: 123). In one of our dossiers, the prisoner had early in his prison career told a psychiatrist about his fantasies about killing people in a wood at the moment of ejaculation. Although he has long admitted that 'I was taking the piss, I made it up', the fantasy finds itself repeated in the dossier and in the prisoner's words, 'I think it's probably the stupidest lie I've ever told in my life. It comes back and haunts me'.

[O]verall they're satisfactory, clearly otherwise we'd be screaming about it... sometimes it's not entirely clear why there's a psychiatric report in one case and not in another, or psychologist. You suspect it's the availability of staff in the individual prisons and the way in which sometimes, say the psychologist...will actually turn up and be questioned and that can be very valuable because you've got a real body of knowledge about an individual. Others, you think, this chap's slipped through the net (independent).

The arrangement, summaries and presentation of reports was unusually good, but individual reports were repetitive, sometimes out-of-date, and their arrival was often late. The quality of individual reports was variable. The dossiers were easy to read, starting with summaries of each report-writer's report and recommendation and an overview, and containing sufficient material to provide a comprehensive picture of the prisoner's index offence, prison career and any work undertaken. They were interesting if somewhat traumatic to read. Reports written by psychiatrists and officers were of more variable quality than some others. Expert witness (especially psychologist) reports and reports written on completion of offending behaviour courses were regarded as especially helpful. Prisoners' own written representations were not always helpful, given the oral hearing. Reports written by individuals with limited contact or knowledge of the prisoner were considered 'a waste of everyone's time' by prisoners but were often treated with more weight by the panel. There were comments made that individual report writers were not always aware of how much weight was given to their report and their recommendations, nor of how important it was that reports directly addressed the question of risk, and provided evidence. Some panel members thought it was difficult to distinguish between 'old' and 'new' or 'irrelevant' and 'relevant' information, and that dossiers should be compiled with these distinctions in mind. Inevitably the management and delivery of external reports was often harder to achieve than internal reports. Prisoners observed that reasons for (especially positive) recommendations were important, in order to make the reports useful to the panel. There were some questions raised about whether the reports actually provided sufficient information of the right type to enable a risk assessment to be made. Some clearer thinking about the sort of reports required and the purpose they were to serve was needed.

Timeliness

I believe that a dossier should have all the reports, complete, up-to-date reports, but that is not very often the case, the late reports come in dribs and drabs (HEO).

Panel members received dossiers about two or three weeks before a hearing, but they were invariably supplemented with (often crucial) late reports at or shortly before the hearing. This resulted in time spent reading before the hearing could start, and sometimes major changes in direction and strategy, where new information came to light. The other problem with timeliness was the inclusion in the dossier of out-of-date reports, so the balance between achieving fully up-to-date material and providing information ahead of the hearing was a difficult one ('you want reports as near to the point of the decision as possible', legal representative). The Secretary of State's view, which was dependent on complete reports, often arrived at or on the morning of the hearing. This made the panel's task (and the roles of Lifer Governor and legal representative) particularly difficult.

The responsibility for the production of timely reports was unclear, as the 'blame' was placed on establishments, on lifer review unit, and on panel secretaries, whose job was to ensure timely delivery:

> ...[I]t's almost as if the prisons have forgotten that the reports have got to go in so much earlier so that there's the full disclosure...And I don't know whether that's a training issue or what really (psychologist).

Late reports and papers were received either on the day or shortly before the panel date in 25 cases; these were mostly psychiatric or psychological reports, including post-treatment psychological assessments. As we noted earlier, the Secretary of State's view was submitted late in 16 cases, again either on the day or shortly before the panel. The late arrival of reports made it very difficult for the prisoner or his representative to prepare their case. Late reports sometimes led to deferral of cases (for about six months) either before, or sometimes at the hearing, wasting public money and risking considerable unfairness to the prisoner. Chasing them was an administrative burden. We were informed that in 60 per cent of DLP cases in 1998, disclosure of full dossiers was achieved before the hearing. We were also encouraged to learn that an auditable standard on the timeliness of submitting reports has recently been introduced.

Deferrals and delays

In our sample of 69 cases, 13 were deferred before the hearing (19% of the cases). Most of these deferrals were due to factors beyond the panel's control, and often occurred because the prisoner wished to complete a course. However, some were related to disputed evidence (or evidence which might have been disputed):

- one case where a key probation witness failed to appear (the case was deferred more than four months)

- one case where the prisoner had a serious adjudication pending (the case was deferred for two months pending the adjudication)
- one case where the prisoner said he wanted legal representation but had failed to contact his solicitor. He complained that he had not been assisted (the case was re-listed four months later).

The question of delay was significant, particularly given that the prisoner only has one right to a challenge to his/her detention every two years from expiry of the tariff. Since a case could not be deferred without the agreement of the prisoner, some respondents suggested that all deferrals 'were at the request of the prisoner'. However, when we explored the reasons for the deferrals, the position was not so straightforward: for example, one reason (apparent in four cases) was to allow the prisoner time to complete a course (for example, SOTP; extended SOTP, and Victim Empathy). There were often delays in achieving a place on the course, so this was only in an indirect sense 'at the request of the prisoner'. Another reason for deferral was that the prisoner was waiting for his 'imminent transfer' to a lower category prison (at least two cases). It was obviously in their interests to move as far as they could before the hearing so that the hearing might 'nudge' them further, but again this raised the question of why they had not already moved before the hearing was listed. The most frequent reason for deferrals was the late arrival of reports: legal representatives applied shortly before the hearing for a deferral since the dossier was incomplete. This was both unfair on the prisoner and wasteful of resources.

From the dossiers, it appeared that in 20 of the 52 cases the DLP took place outside the agreed timetable. Whilst this was no more than five months delay in 17 of these cases, the remaining three had been delayed nine months, 13 months and 21 months respectively. One of these concerned a man who had been released in 1983, but had been recalled in 1990. At a DLP in 1992, the panel had recommended his transfer to Category C with a 12 month review after the date of transfer, which had taken place in April 1993. Since then, the case was regularly deferred whilst he underwent behaviour modification therapy, which then required a PPG (penile plethysmograph) to see whether the work had been successful. A panel met in January 1999 but was again deferred following the late submission of a psychologist's report. It was again deferred in May 1999 for the reports to be re-written, ready for hearing in July 1999, at which it was recommended that he should move to open conditions. The timetable of the DLP process seemed to have fitted uncomfortably with the Prison Service's own timetable of treatment for this prisoner.

Delays also appeared to happen because of the bureaucratic constraints of the DLP process. The Parole Board fixed a provisional timetable for hearings some eight or nine months in advance, on the assumption that the prisoner would remain in the same prison. There was evidence that a prisoner might not be moved on to another prison during that time, since he was waiting for a DLP. There were dangers that the prisoner's progress would freeze pending the next hearing. The DLP might well help to 'nudge' some prisoners through the lifer system, but it seemed also inadvertently to slow them down.

Differences between first oral recall hearings and ordinary DLPs

In our study, we observed five panels hearing recall cases at their first oral hearings post-recall. Three other observed cases involved prisoners who had previously been released and recalled. Two other (non-observed) cases involved recalled lifers. Those who had been recalled spent long periods in prison following their recall between three and 11 years in our sample. At subsequent DLPs for recalled prisoners there was no significant difference between hearings and those of non-recalled prisoners. This section will therefore concentrate on the differences between proceedings at the first recall DLP and others.

Practical differences

Prisoners who were recalled by the Home Secretary under s32(2) of the Crime (Sentences) Act 1997 (see Appendix 1) were recalled to the nearest local prison. The prisoner was likely to stay there until after his recall had been confirmed both by the Parole Board at a paper hearing in London, and at the subsequent first full DLP. They were therefore likely to be held for a number of months in a prison which was not designed to take lifers. Our five recalled prisoners had each been in a local prison for between five and 12 months since they had been recalled. The length of time was influenced by the practical problems of arranging a hearing, and the availability of the necessary players in the hearing. During this time the local prison was merely 'holding' the prisoner: little seemed to be done by way of assessment or report writing.

We observed recall hearings in five different local prisons[44]. Since these prisons do not host regular DLPs, the practical arrangements tended to be less successful: the hearings were held in unsuitable rooms, for example. Panels were more likely to suffer intrusive disruptions (telephones ringing, noise outside, people entering the room). Prison staff were less aware of the implications of holding a recall case. For example, in one prison no arrangements had been made for lunch for the panel despite the fact the hearing was scheduled to last all day, and in another the prison staff interrupted the hearing to insist (unsuccessfully) that the prisoner be returned to his wing for lunch at a time to suit the convenience of the establishment.

---

44. Norwich, Wormwood Scrubs, Bedford, Leeds and Leicester.

Evidential differences

The main difference in a recall hearing was the nature of the evidence. The prisoner was likely to be challenging the reasons for his recall. Hearings were generally longer than other DLPs, and witnesses were always called (see Figure 4.1).

We saw some uncertainty on the part of panels as to what exactly their function was in recall cases. In one case, the judge carefully read to his other panel members at the pre-panel discussion, and again to all the participants at the hearing itself, para 5B.2 of the Parole Board's Policy and Procedures Manual:

> When considering representations against recall, the panel should primarily consider whether the representations alter the basis of the original decision to recall. The panel should not routinely undertake a full risk assessment. Where representations provide no information or evidence which casts doubt on the basis of the original decision, the recall decisions should be confirmed.

It seemed unlikely that this is appropriate guidance. The Court of Appeal has held that the Board should apply the same test on recalls as it does on earlier reviews[45]. It was therefore required to assess whether 'it is no longer necessary for the protection of the public that the prisoner should be confined'. Since the main argument before the panel was likely to be whether the recall can be justified, without the benefit of up-to-date reports, the task of assessing risk was more difficult. We observed that it was less directly discussed.

What is the evidence?

Whilst the evidence at an ordinary DLP was largely based on the reports in the dossier, which were written by prison staff who know the prisoner well, the emphasis in a recall case was on the matters which led to recall. In the recall cases which we observed, the written evidence of the probation service was entirely about the recall, and the justifications for it. The dossier did not usually include any release plan.

The evidence in a recall case was often open to challenge and interpretation. The supervision arrangements had broken down: the panel was perhaps looking at risk management rather than assessing risk. For example, in our sample, two prisoners had been recalled because of concern which had arisen due to one or two bouts of drinking, one because of drug abuse, and another because of concern about his 'unreasonable behaviour'. The only witnesses called, apart from the prisoner, the probation officer and the assistant chief probation officer, were family members and close friends called on behalf of

---

45. See *R v Parole Board, ex p Watson* [1996] 1 WLR 906; [1996] 2 All ER 641, discussed at pages 14/15.

the prisoner. The evidence of the probation officers was therefore either to be accepted or rejected but was not supported by the evidence of others 'at risk' from the inappropriate behaviour. The evidence of the probation officers was 'hearsay': evidence given by people who had formed opinions sometimes at third hand:

> At Mr X's recall much turned on his relationship with a young woman. The probation officer admitted under examination that much of her written report was inaccurate:
> When I wrote it there was very little hard evidence available. I was asked to write it over lunchtime for that afternoon. PC X was off sick so I couldn't check facts with her. Lots in it was not true... There had been a strong suggestion from the police that he had been paying her unwanted attention, but that's not true. She chose to spend lots of time with him.
> The judge became exasperated: How much of what you are telling us is tittle tattle?

The main evidence at an ordinary DLP where release was a realistic option was the release plan. Here, where the panel was meant to be considering release, they often have no release plan to consider.

Procedural differences
At all the recall cases we observed, the Secretary of State was represented by someone from LRU, not someone from the prison. Thus the representative was more experienced in legal procedures, and would play a more active role examining witnesses than was usual. The Secretary of State's view was not circulated in advance.

What factors count?
On a recall the panel was clearly influenced by evidence of the prisoner's ability to survive in the community. Discussions concentrated on recent factual evidence on his/her life in the community, in particular the breakdown in the relationship with the probation service. Earlier prison reports were not regarded as relevant.

Outcomes
All the recall hearings we attended resulted in the recall being confirmed. Panels varied as to whether they made specific recommendations; in three of the five cases a specific recommendation was made, one for a move to open conditions, one for a move to a Resettlement Prison and one to another named prison. Given that the panel is making a decision on the facts (in our cases, believing the probation service's version of events and not the prisoner's), it was surprising that the decision letters do not give fuller reasons.

Given that no panel would direct release unless it was convinced that it was safe to do so, it was hardly surprising that the recall is confirmed when the panel was offered no adequate release plan. The fact that the relationship with the probation officer had broken down also militated against the likelihood of release. In one case a panel member specifically asked the assistant chief probation officer whether if the panel released the prisoner he would be supervised by the same officer. He gave an ambivalent answer: 'we'd review the situation'. Another panel member commented during the discussion that he liked this question because he too was concerned about the quality of supervision: 'She wasn't very convincing… her contact with him certainly left something to be desired'. We were left with the feeling that the panel's doubts about the probation officer may have helped tip the balance towards confirming the recall.

Are any of the differences defensible?

Many of the differences between recalls and ordinary DLPs flowed simply from the fact that they concerned prisoners who had been released and then recalled: they were at a different and more difficult stage in their life sentence. The differences also flowed from the nature of the evidence on risk, which stemmed from their time in the community. The panel was being asked to do two different things in the hearing: both to confirm the recall (i.e. to confirm that the recall had been necessary to protect the public) and to consider whether it was still necessary for the protection of the public that the prisoner should be confined. The panel often concentrated on the first part of the question, and did not have adequate material to make a sound judgement on the second. We recommend that the two decisions should be considered separately[46]. The current recall system was widely considered to be unfair. Given the significance of the human rights issues (and the small numbers of prisoners) involved, we would suggest that greater priority should be given to recall hearings.

Summary

This chapter has described the DLP process and raised a number of issues arising from our observations of it. We were impressed by the seriousness with which panel members undertook their task and by the inherently difficult nature of the task they faced. Late papers detracted from the otherwise impressive nature of the decision-making process, and there was room for greater intervention by the Chair at the pre-panel preparation stage. The hearings themselves were thorough, usually quite formal, but reasonably friendly. The procedures we observed were quite consistent. The style or tone varied according to the

---

46. Though we are conscious that if this were to happen on separate occasions it would introduce an even greater delay into a system which already appears unduly tardy.

manner of the judge in the Chair. The deliberations were quite swift, and concentrated on the outcome and the reasons to appear in the letter. Sometimes there was insufficient explicit attention given to the nature and level of the risk posed. Hearings were often deferred or delayed. This was unfair to the prisoner and wasteful of resources. Recall cases were unusual and had a distinct purpose. There seemed to be two purposes in some tension: to confirm the original recall decision and to assess the current level of risk. Recalled prisoners were 'in limbo', often inappropriately housed for long periods in local prisons, until the hearing took place.

5   Roles and perspectives

Introduction

This chapter considers the roles played by participants in the DLP process and the perspectives they had on the themes explored in our research. We draw mainly on our interview data for this part of our account, although the way we have organised the material is inevitably informed by the observational and other aspects of the research.

The role of the judge

All hearings were chaired by a judge, unlike 'paper only' Mandatory Lifer Panels, where all three panel members took it in turns to take the lead on the different cases under review. This was perhaps an inevitable consequence of the European Court of Human Rights ruling in *Thynne*[47] (that a discretionary lifer is entitled to have the lawfulness of his or her detention reviewed by a court or tribunal which is independent of the executive) but it also served to add a certain legal formality to proceedings.

As we explained in Chapter Four, the judge received the dossier a few weeks before their fellow panel members and were asked to give pre-hearing directions. We have not observed what happens at this stage, but the role of the judge was to give directions regarding the attendance of witnesses and the submission of evidence. It was also their opportunity to point out any difficulty which was likely to arise if the LLO who was to represent the Secretary of State at the hearing had written a report which conflicted with the Secretary of State's view. However, since the Secretary of State's view often did not arrive until shortly before the hearing, a direction on potential conflict could not then happen until the last minute.

The main role of the judge at the hearing itself was to chair proceedings. Thus, they generally agreed the procedure, especially the order of the witnesses, with the parties. Normally this would be discussed very briefly, if at all, with the other panel members prior to the hearing. Judges were more likely to agree a suitable procedure with the legal representative. Some judges took the lead in questioning witnesses; others left it to their colleagues, simply 'mopping up at the end', asking the questions which they felt had not been adequately explored by their colleagues.

---

47. See page 11.

We asked interviewees whether it was essential that the panel should be chaired by a judge. Responses varied, though a majority felt that it was important: partly because the law required it, and partly because their skills as judges were useful in chairing the hearing. Those who doubted whether it was necessary for a judge to chair proceedings stressed that it was human qualities such as empathy, fairness and consistency which were more important than the attribute of simply being a judge. All the prisoners said they felt the panel should be chaired by a judge: a judge was seen to be more objective and independent than a psychiatrist or a politician. This is significant, since it suggests that prisoners are implicitly backing a formal separation of powers between executive and judiciary.

The judge set the tone, introducing the various participants at the beginning of the hearing. Most made a serious attempt to help the prisoner relax, but this was not universally the case:

We've had a few incidents with the judges being frankly quite rude (lifer liaison officer).

The judge, he'd only just retired from the bench so it was his first panel; he was rather abrupt, insisted that I faced him and looked at him at all times. Even if I glanced at my notes or anything he would say 'Would you mind looking at me please'. I felt that I was being suppressed in putting my side of the argument (prisoner).

The cases where the judges are not particularly good, it's not because they are trying to be bad, it's just their background, the sort of people they are (legal representative).

When he was questioning me about why it was important about whether I was going to take drugs or don't take drugs outside and he looked at me like I was a tramp. Whatever I said I was going to condemn myself. I felt my openness was being held against me (prisoner).

Perhaps it goes without saying that the judge who appeared more informal and relaxed was not necessarily a 'soft touch':

Some of the most gentle judges are the most lethal (judge).

The judges, being more accustomed to an accusatorial-style court process, were not always comfortable with a more inquisitorial process. Generally, they were keen to keep a distance and a formality in the proceedings:

I am wary of entering the arena too much, for fear of being perceived as partisan, by the person who is applying to me and my colleagues for a recommendation or a direction. I think it's important that we don't appear too inquisitorial... It's simply that my training of 45 years at the Bar has been against entering into the arena. But I can quite see that wearing my Parole Board hat I must be more willing to do so (judge).

Judges enjoyed the help of experienced lawyers:

On a reps [representations] against recall, I have had a highly competent Treasury Counsel who's done a terrific job. They have made our task easier. They've combed the dossier in a way that a highly paid barrister should do so. Take us to the heart of it (judge).

When it came to drafting the reasons (the letter to the prisoner), in most cases the judges took the leading role. This was accepted by the other panel members who seemed to defer to the judge's skills in draughtsmanship or who simply acknowledged that team drafting was time-consuming. However, as we have already noted, the other panel members would contribute in various ways. The Rules provide that the judge should sign the written record of the decision. In practice what this meant was that they signed the draft at the panel hearing; the letter sent to the prisoner was signed by a member of the Parole Board secretariat.

So judges played an important and effective role in chairing panels and brought to them (on the whole) a formality which was required of the process. Most achieved this in a friendly manner.

The role of the psychiatrist

Well, I suppose over and above being a member of the parole board I think there is a common theme which runs across all the three members: assessing risk to the public, listening to the prisoner and the representative, reading all the papers, asking the questions. When there is clear evidence of mental disorder, I think it is my role to make sure these have been addressed, and also when release is planned, proper post-release supervision is in place, and to test their resolve... and that's if you like the added value I can give to the panel. Other than that I would like to think that I'm there as a lay person as well as an expert (psychiatrist).

Despite the guidelines issued by the Home Secretary in 1992 (see page 12) a psychiatrist sat on every panel. The part they played in proceedings varied, partly according to the nature of the prisoner and his/her offence; and partly according to the nature of the psychiatrist. The role of the psychiatrist was a delicate one. A significant number of discretionary life sentence prisoners suffer from, or have suffered from, mental health problems or psychiatric disorders. In these cases, the psychiatrist often took the lead amongst panel members, certainly in asking the searching and more difficult questions about motivation, thoughts and feelings. We were interested to compare the DLP process, where the panel member will not have interviewed the prisoner in advance of the hearing (indeed one psychiatrist was excluded from a panel at the request of a solicitor since he had examined the prisoner much earlier in his prison career), with the procedure at Mental Health Review Tribunals where the psychiatric member interviews the patient in advance[48].

Different psychiatrists perceived their role differently and played it to varying degrees of success. Where there was no psychiatric or medical evidence, some psychiatrists chose to take very little active role in proceedings. Others would nonetheless play an active role, seeing themselves as a full and perhaps 'independent' member of the panel. Several interviewees suggested that it might not be necessary to have a psychiatrist on the panel in cases where the prisoner did not have a history of mental illness, particularly in many HMP cases. We found their role useful. Some in particular contributed a valuable 'voice of reason' based on their familiarity with difficult behaviour, their understanding of mental health settings, of treatment prospects and of risk. We witnessed several 'changes of direction' at hearings because a psychiatrist had provided a counterbalance to the other panel members' assumptions. On the other hand, we occasionally witnessed what appeared as a full 'clinical interview' conducted before the panel. It was more appropriate, given the public nature of the event, when psychiatrists drew on psychiatric reports, elaborating on them and asking relevant and revealing questions, often of a broader nature, at the hearing.

Most of our respondents pointed out the special nature of the discretionary lifer population, arguing that the sex offender and arsonist offenders required a psychiatric specialist with relevant (preferably, forensic) experience. Occasionally irrelevant experience (a special interest in a barely related subject) interfered with the dialogue, and took the questioning in an inappropriate direction. We felt that it was appropriate to have a psychiatrist member, partly to explore issues raised in psychiatric reports but also to assess the prisoner at the hearing and to add an important and specifically clinical dimension to the decision-making process. There could be better 'quality control', as several of our respondents argued.

---

48. This has the advantage that the psychiatrist has been able to make their own clinical diagnosis, but the disadvantage that they may have over-dominant influence on the panel: see Holloway, 2000.

The role of the 'independent member'[49]

It was interesting to learn during the research process (it was mentioned often) that independent members who were selected to sit on DLPs were an 'elite' or special group, who often had considerable experience before being selected for the task, from the pool of Parole Board members. Several non-DLP members expressed interest (and some impatience!) in joining this 'privileged' group, who took on this most difficult and interesting role.

The role played by independent members varied enormously: and varied at different stages in the proceedings. Some played a full and equal role, asking lots of questions and influencing the topics raised. Some were quiet during the hearing but then played a fuller part in discussions. Some saw their role as a representative of the public, interfering only when they thought the professionals were over-stepping the mark:

> We as independents always see ourselves as a third arm...it's having that very practical approach – you know we're in the real world out there (independent).

This lay role was welcomed by the other participants:

> I think professionals can be too clever for their own good sometimes (psychiatrist).

> There should be more peasants like me on the Parole Board! (lifer governor).

The degree of influence of independent members was a reflection of the individuals involved. Full-time members of the Board, senior probation officers, and those who had been professionally involved with the parole process were assertive and were listened to. Other professionals (solicitors, people in business, etc.) were equally full participants. We did hear that the independent members differed more than other members in this respect, and other panel members seemed to prefer those independent members who behaved as equal parties to the decision. 'Experience of life' and (to some extent) 'experience of prison' were seen as desirable assets, and those members who were in the Probation Service clearly drew on their experience usefully. Like the psychiatrists and judges, they were often able to comment on the competence of their colleagues who had written reports in the dossier or who were to play a part in the release plan. Independent members tended to sit on fewer panels (because there were more of them) which meant that their experience was less. Their involvement was seen as symbolically important ('to be joe public'). They were

49. We are conscious that this is a misleading title. All members of the Parole Board are independent. However, we use the term since it is the term used within the Parole Board (and includes the criminologists and probation officers who also sit as the third panel member).

practical and (in theory) representative of the community. As we argue below, the three panel members were a good balance, requiring different professional and lay perspectives to be reconciled.

The role of the panel

Even though the individual members of the panel often had different and separate roles, they worked together, asking each other questions and challenging each other's views, in the pre-panel discussion as much as in the post-hearing decision-making phase of the process. By sharing their ideas, their views evolved and changed: we have given examples of the process of negotiation in Chapter Four.

At the hearing, they shared the questioning of the witnesses:

> So an ideal panel is really getting maximum input, psychiatric input and the maximum lay input and the judge really just standing back and hammering in on the areas that haven't been covered (judge).

We were impressed that panels never asked questions for the sake of asking questions: only when it was useful to get an answer. Since the independent member was normally asked by the judge if he/she had any questions only after the psychiatrist, it was not surprising that independents had fewer questions: their questions had already been asked.

Sometimes one member took a more dominant role, or another was unduly silent, but each panel functioned as a team. It is difficult to make generalisations about who controlled proceedings: it varied according to the case, and the make up of the panel. Panel members were not reluctant to criticise their colleagues – there were good members, and not so good members:

> You do get people who cruise, who can produce something on a flick through the papers, get a superficial view and not do very much (judge).

> Some of those on the induction course with me would take a lot of inducting (judge).

Three was widely respected as a quorum. A few panel members would have welcomed a fourth member, but none wished to reduce to a panel of two.

When it came to drafting written reasons, panels adopted different patterns of drafting. Judges tended to take the lead. Psychiatrists were normally either very involved, or quite remote from the process. Most independent members played an active, but supporting, role.

The role of the panel was clearly to assess and make a decision on risk, but also to act as a post-tariff safeguard for the prisoner. Panels were conscious that they were not there to be a complaints adjudicator ('we're not some kind of godfather, (judge)), yet they seemed to find it difficult not to get drawn into wider issues:

> I find it very difficult to understand how prisons or how the Prison Service works in the Cat A and B ... I do wonder about fairness, it's not our role to criticise and ask is it fair or unfair, but it doesn't stop us making a judgement. And I do question why some people are in A and some people are in B and sometimes how on earth someone got to D. So I won't know because it's not our role to be told, but sometimes it doesn't stop me wondering (independent).

This 'wondering' was done out loud in panel discussions. We were not surprised that it led panels beyond the strict letter of their terms of reference, and involved them in issues relating to the prisoner's management (see our discussions of the terms of reference, later in this chapter; see also Chapter Six on the dual function of the DLP).

The role the panel performed was the conservative task of carefully assessing risk with a view to protecting the public (see later in this chapter). They could have interpreted their role far more radically, challenging 'the State' to justify the continuing detention of the prisoner (see Chapter Six: we return in the final chapter to consider legal presumptions).

The role of the panel secretary

The panel secretary job description specified that they should:

- ensure that all panels are conducted effectively by the due date, in accordance with internal instructions, and provide sound, considered and thorough advice and guidance to the panel members, particularly in respect of drafting their decisions and recommendations

- ensure the efficient preparation of cases due to be considered by lifer panels including the issue of prompt and accurate responses to all written and telephone enquiries from solicitors and the Prison Service, and offering sound advice to panel chairmen in the preparation of their directions
- ensure the practical arrangements for the oral hearings are efficient, and take proper account of budget implications and that details of arrangements are conveyed to all parties
- ensure panel decisions adhere to current guidelines and directions and are circulated within the required time-scale. Deal effectively and as promptly as possible with any enquiries resulting from those decisions.

The wording of this job description highlighted some of the anomalies in the role of panel secretary. The panel secretaries we observed were successful in achieving the logistical demands of their job, arranging rooms, lunch and so on. However, there was wide variation in the way in which they interpreted their role in a number of critical areas:

- providing sound, considered and thorough advice to panel members. Some panel secretaries became over-involved in the decision-making process, contributing their own views on the evidence during the deliberation ('it seems that fires are still his main interest'; 'I thought he handled the doctor very well'; 'I don't think he's got any empathy'). Occasionally the extent to which they intervened seemed to displease some panel members; others seemed to welcome their involvement.

- advising panel members on drafting of letters. Panel secretaries had very different understandings of the extent to which they should involve themselves in the drafting process. Some would contribute nothing and indeed might have been out of the room, arranging tea or lunch throughout the drafting process. Others would suggest better or more appropriate wording:

It would be useful for a future panel if you said..

No, the panel understands that in open conditions you will...

Perhaps you should mention the successful home leaves.

To avoid a judicial review, perhaps you should mention the drugs...

It was usual for them to be present during the final 'read through' of the draft. They also had to ensure they could decipher the judge's handwriting.

It is difficult for us to comment on whether panel secretaries were adequately providing sound advice to judges in the preparation of the directions, though, as we have said elsewhere, this seemed to be an area which could be managed more effectively.

The role of witnesses

Who were the witnesses?

Witnesses were called in 28 of the 52 cases observed: home probation officers were called most frequently, followed by psychologists, prison probation officers, and family and friends[50]. There seemed to be no consistent pattern as to which witnesses were called. The prisoner or his/her legal representative made most of the decisions, sanctioned by the judge in the pre-hearing directions. It was not clear from the observational part of our study whether the Secretary of State or his/her representative ever took the initiative to call specific witnesses. In interviews, it was explained that the Secretary of State did not often call witnesses, because 'the other side' did it. The Secretary of State only called a witness when there had been subsequent developments since the report was written or some other matter which was particularly sensitive about risk. It seemed to be the habit of most judges to allow the parties to call whichever witnesses they chose (within reason)[51]. We were not aware of any examples of judges specifically requesting witnesses, apart from cases where the previous panel had requested specific reports to be carried out. Legal representatives had some difficulties adapting to the inquisitorial nature of the hearing:

---

50. See Figure 5.1.
51. Supplementary guidance to the Parole Rules 1997 specifies:
   Applications to call witnesses are normally granted, not least because to refuse an application (for which reasons must be given in writing) tends to make the prisoner perceive that justice has not been done so that he is dissatisfied even before the hearing begins. However, in considering applications panel chairmen must have regard to the length of hearings, strains upon the Prison Service and costs. The general practice in non-recall cases is as follows:
   ● witnesses not on the dossier... always grant
   ● witnesses on the dossier who are favourable to the prisoner.. grant only if it is indicated the witness can add orally to the statements in the dossier
   ● witnesses in the dossier unfavourable to the prisoner whom the prisoner's representative wishes to challenge.. usually grant.
   In recall cases the same general practice applies but panel chairmen should additionally encourage the attendance of witnesses who can speak to the primary facts relating to the recall. The Board considers it important that the Secretary of State's case for recalling the prisoner should not be only on paper in the dossier when it is hotly challenged (as it usually is) in the flesh by the prisoner. It is normal for the panel chairman to request the attendance of home probation officers should they not have been called by either party.

We're calling (the psychologist) but she's not our witness (legal representative).

He is only here as he heard about this panel by accident, but he's not strictly entitled to give evidence as he hasn't written a report (legal representative, of a probation officer).

Other witnesses were specifically called although they had not written a report (for example, the Head of Activities and Services at one prison was called because the Secretary of State's representative felt that he could give helpful information about the drug testing regime in this particular prison).

Figure 5.1: *Witnesses called*

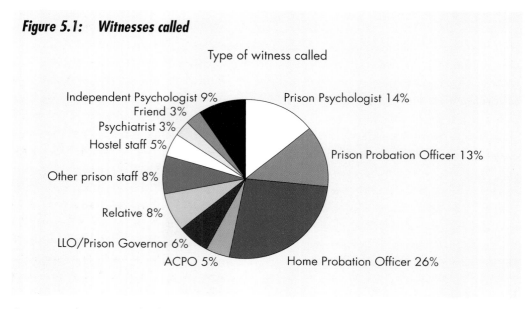

Type of witness called

Independent Psychologist 9%
Friend 3%
Psychiatrist 3%
Hostel staff 5%
Other prison staff 8%
Relative 8%
LLO/Prison Governor 6%
ACPO 5%
Prison Psychologist 14%
Prison Probation Officer 13%
Home Probation Officer 26%

Some people came to the hearing uncertain whether they would in fact be witnesses. In one case, it seemed accidental that one particular officer was observing. He was then called as a witness, and it was his personal support which seemed to swing the panel in favour of recommending a move to open conditions. In another case, a senior probation officer was asked by the judge if she was observing or was a witness. She replied that she was primarily observing, but would be happy to help if so required. Sometimes the judge would ask the legal representative whether they were calling a particular observer. One answered:

No, that won't be necessary as you have her statement. She is just here for support (legal representative).

Other observers who could have been useful were not called: for example, in one case both the probation officer and the drugs counsellor were present but were not called. Whilst it may have made sense from the prisoner's point of view not to call them as they might have said things which were not in his interest, it was somewhat surprising. This example also raises the question of confidentiality: prisoners were anxious about admitting things to staff if this means that these admissions might appear unexpectedly in the evidence. For example, a prisoner may be honest with his alcohol or drugs counsellor: it should be made clear to him whether or not this information will be treated with confidence.

Our conclusions about witnesses was that they played a very influential role but that their appearance seemed somewhat haphazard.

The prisoner

What was the role of the prisoner at the hearing? Strictly (and legally) speaking, the prisoner was the key witness. Observers of the social practice of a hearing might argue conversely that the prisoner is the key subject of the hearing and that the prisoner cannot be a 'witness' at his or her own 'trial'. The prisoner stands accused of 'being risky'. His or her role at the hearing (assisted by the legal representative) is to persuade the panel that his/her level of risk is sufficiently reduced to move on (or out). Should the 'burden of proof' rest with the prisoner? Or should it rest with the State (or the panel)? We return to these conceptual uncertainties in our conclusions.

Formally speaking, solicitors called prisoners to give evidence at hearings and often led the questioning. Prisoners gave evidence (answered questions) at every hearing. In one case, the solicitor said he would not be calling the prisoner. The judge then asked the psychiatrist to ask the prisoner some questions. It was the panel's task (and not the task of the legal representative) to establish the level of risk and satisfy themselves as to the prisoner's readiness to move on.

Thus in every panel which the prisoner attended, he or she contributed in some way to the discussion. What varied was the manner in which the prisoner gave evidence. A majority of legal representatives took the prisoner through a lengthy series of questions; others preferred to let the panel ask their own questions first. Many prisoners were extremely nervous, particularly at the beginning of a hearing or when difficult territory was broached: we observed several prisoners shaking, and two crying. One told us that it was much worse than the trial he had faced years earlier:

It's just the pressure; there's so much pressure. It's supposed to be quite informal and they put you at your ease, and in some ways it is. I remember going in and looking at their faces and the smiles on their faces... but as it got into it, it got serious and I felt like they were bending forward and looking at me and I thought 'oh god I can't take any more of this', you know... (prisoner).

There was no hiding from the event: the prisoner was directly opposite the panel across a table, and the panel asked deeply searching and personal questions. The majority of prisoners were treated very sympathetically by the panels, especially at the beginning when they were encouraged to try and relax, feel comfortable and so on. Some panel members pushed very hard. Some judges asked complicated or lengthy questions, or threw many questions at speed. Psychiatrists elicited information successfully, but sometimes at a high price to the prisoner who was left emotionally fraught. Participants commented that some psychiatrists appeared to have 'fixations' of their own: asking questions on sadism or masturbation, for example, when these issues were not obviously relevant.

The prisoner's role was pivotal, and was assisted by good, realistic legal representation. Some prisoners participated more than others. A few may have been disadvantaged by their appearance before the panel, if they betrayed a lack of understanding, or a lack of willingness to take on the panel's interpretation of events.

Psychiatrists and psychologists

We found no pattern to help us understand when experts would be called in person. Indeed, it seemed slightly random who turned up at the hearing. If one report was out of step with the others (for example, more cautious), then it was likely that the legal representative would call them to give evidence, in order to challenge the report. Successful and assertive 'cross-examination' of psychologists was an important influence on the panel's decision to direct release in two cases.

We became aware of the small professional world in which these witnesses worked. Comments on the credibility of the witnesses were not unusual:

I'm very impressed by Dr X's report. Do you know Dr X?

Mr X is always so cautious, that when he recommends release I'll sit up and listen, or (the opposite) Dr X always has a soft spot for these guys.

Mr X has an interest in filling places on his programmes (throwing doubt on the credibility of the witness).

The psychiatric world seemed particularly intimate: in one case, the panel commented that it seemed odd that the Prison Service psychiatrist was from the same unit as the prisoner's own psychiatrist. And occasionally the questioning of a psychiatrist witness by the psychiatrist panel member seemed to resemble professional jousting rather than a search for understanding. Certain key experts sometimes appeared for the Prison Service and sometimes for the prisoner.

We were impressed by the panel's approach to specialist reports. They were discriminating, and robust. They chose between poor evidence and competent evidence, in a few cases going against the recommendation of a specialist report writer if they felt that the evidence was thin. Of the nine cases in our sample who were released, five had received positive recommendations from psychologists. In two cases no recommendation had been made; in one a further risk assessment had been called for and in one there was no psychologist's report.

Home probation officers

A panel only once directed that a prisoner should be released without having seen the home probation officer. One case had to be deferred because of the non-attendance of the home probation officer. As the judge put it, when he was frustrated that the panel had to defer :

> We like to question the licence holder. It's all very well for these people to say they are sick. The safety of the public rests in the net of the probation service (judge).

At one hearing the panel was delighted to see the hostel worker as well as the probation officer. Whilst this might have been seen as a waste of public money, it was a shrewd move on the part of the solicitor or probation officer to ask the hostel worker to come: he was an impressive witness, and gave the panel more confidence in their decision to release. Panels were interested in the management of risk: questions to home probation officers sometimes suggested that it was the home probation officer who was being assessed and not only the prisoner:

> Independent: If you found Mr X was using alcohol what would your view be?
> Home probation officer: I would treat it seriously as a breach of licence and it might well result in a recall.

The role of Secretary of State's view, and of his representative

Secretary of State's view

The Secretary of State's view was presented at the hearing by the Secretary of State's representative, but had been received in written form, frequently only shortly before the hearing, as we indicated in Chapter Three. It was often late, and frequently non-specific: in seven of our cases, the Secretary of State offered no view (in a majority of cases, because of the late arrival of reports). The Secretary of State's view was prepared in Lifer Review Unit usually at HEO level, and approved by a Grade 7 civil servant. When DLPs were first introduced, the dossiers did not include a view from the Secretary of State, but the inclusion of a formal 'Secretary of State's view' has evolved over the years as a response to questions asked by the panel of the presenting officer.

If the Secretary of State's view was to the effect that the prisoner should be released or transferred to open conditions, LRU have to seek prior Ministerial approval. It is outside the scope of this study to examine the extent to which this requirement encourages caution from LRU.

Some interviewees suggested that the Secretary of State's view was not useful, and should be abolished. It was clear that panels did not have high regard for the quality of the Secretary of State's view: comments were made even during hearings that it was 'formulaic', and drawn up by 'some faceless civil servant', or 'that mysterious man upstairs'. Some prisoners thought that the Secretary of State, who had not met the prisoner, was not entitled to a view. When the Secretary of State had no view, this was irritating for all concerned:

> From a personal point of view I was extremely miffed when about 18 months ago I sat round that table and read out the Secretary of State's view, which was that there was no view, and the judge just put his glasses on the end of his nose and lambasted me as the Secretary of State.... Either every DLP has no (Secretary of State's) opinion, so that the panel knows that's where the lifer governor is coming from, or they do give an opinion. I feel quite strongly about that (lifer governor).

> It just seems really stupid. I mean they've got reports, I mean just say something. It's taken them a year.. they just wasn't making a decision. I just thought it's absurd. It's absolutely stupid (prisoner).

The meaning of the phrase, 'the Secretary of State is not in a position to provide a view' was not clear. To many legal representatives and prisoners it did not imply 'the Secretary of

State has not had the opportunity to study the dossier' or that late reports had not allowed time for proper consideration; rather they felt that it meant, 'I can't stop this one being released but I can't actually be seen to support the release of this triple rapist'.

As we have indicated, a major complaint was the lateness with which the Secretary of State's view was received:

> I only got the Secretary of State's view in the panel. It was blinding. If I had seen it before, I would have changed my plea (prisoner).

> It comes very often a day before the hearing. Absolutely outrageous (legal representative).

There was also frank complaint about some of the Secretary of State's views being routinised and out-of-date e.g. the Secretary of State's frequent recommendation of PRES (the pre-release employment scheme) which panel members believed to be more or less non-existent; they felt free to accept that a release plan was better suited to the prisoner's management than would be a move to PRES. In six cases the Secretary of State's view disagreed with the majority of the report writers: he took a more cautious approach to either release or a move to open conditions. In five of these six cases, the panel disregarded the Secretary of State's view.

However, the Secretary of State's view seemed to us to have two major functions. First, the panel often referred to it as they finalised the decision letter, responding specifically to aspects of the Secretary of State's view. Secondly, when it was received on time, it was useful to legal representatives as they prepared the case for the prisoner. It may have been particularly important in cases where the prisoner was not seeking release but sought some kind of progress through the system: it allowed the legal representative a clearer idea of the issues which they need to address at the hearing. We return to the relationship between the Prison Service and the Parole Board in Chapter Six.

The Secretary of State's representative

The Secretary of State's representative at the hearing was usually the lifer governor or lifer liaison officer. The impact of the representative on proceedings was frequently minor, though in some cases, where the representative participated actively in the hearing they had an important impact. However, most representatives followed the written Guidance issued to Secretary of State's representatives:

The role of the presenting governor is not to act as a lawyer might in court. It is not for him or her to seek to undermine the prisoner's case or to try to argue the panel round to a particular decision for or against release...: It may of course be the case that the presenter can use his or her expertise and knowledge of the system to challenge the prisoner's side on any claims which might be regarding suitability for release. But, generally speaking, this will be a matter for the panel (Page, 1998).

This Guidance, developed when DLPs were first set up, reflected the expectation of the Prison Service at that time: that panels would ask their own questions, would make their own enquiries of witnesses, and would not rely on the Secretary of State's representative to take an active role. The majority of Secretary of State's representatives appeared comfortable with this role: happy to help the panel, but remaining detached from the questioning. Even some of the more experienced Secretary of State's representatives appeared surprised when invited to ask questions or to get involved:

Judge: Do you want to ask any questions, Mr X?
Secretary of State rep: Who? Me? No, no questions!

It was not an easy experience:

I've sometimes had to tangle with a prisoner with not only a solicitor but a barrister as well. Well, for goodness sake, I haven't had the training or the background or the education that they've had and it can be well embarrassing sometimes (Secretary of State's representative).

The less experienced varied considerably in their role and impact: one first time representative barely spoke, and confessed to being terrified. Another took on the role of advocate with enthusiasm and her advocate-like approach to the questioning made a significant impact on the panel. The prisoner knew this:

She's put in an impossible position, right. She's got to represent the Home Secretary's view, based on very little knowledge of the details. I mean, she had 24 hours to scan up on this. In fact I had to get a photocopy of the procedure for her.... I think she took a very harsh stance to support his point of view and whilst I can see that she's got to do that, that's her role, that's exactly why she's there I felt that perhaps it was a little overdone.. My understanding of her role on this board was simply to make known the views of the Home Secretary, not to expand upon them in any way shape or form. I may be wrong in my interpretation of DLP and the roles, but... she did far greater than that which I didn't think was needed. I think she'll be the deciding factor, for sure. She emphasised the need to stay in closed conditions two or three times and it's unfair that someone who doesn't know me is able to do that (prisoner).

Panels seemed to be more comfortable with those who took an active role: this confirmed the view expressed to us that it was the judicial preference for an adversarial format which has led to a pressure for greater involvement of the Secretary of State's representative (see Chapter Six on inquisitorial and accusatorial tensions). But it was not only judges who preferred this:

[The Secretary of State's representative's role] is to intelligently examine the information and the data in the dossier and to give a view of what is the safe approach from the point of view of the public alone. They should really be interested in the protection of the public to a much greater extent than the rights of the individual... They shouldn't just be parroting a safe line (psychiatrist).

In two cases, the judge had directed that the Lifer Governor should not be the Secretary of State's representative since his report was not in line with the Secretary of State's view. In one case this led to an angry exchange between the Lifer Governor and the judge: the prison had only heard the afternoon prior to the hearing that the lifer governor was not to be permitted to represent the Secretary of State. He let us know when we arrived how frustrated he had felt by this decision, and how unfair he thought it was that the new Governor 5, who had never had the opportunity previously to observe a panel, had had to take over at such short notice. He took this matter up with the judge, who tried to be placatory, but there was clearly a strength of feeling on both sides.[52]

The Secretary of State ought to ensure that somebody competent represents him. Usually it's left to the lifer governor and often the lifer governor's views don't coincide with the Secretary of State's views. The lifer governor may be only too keen to see the prisoner out of this establishment, he's sick to death of him, whereas the Secretary of State concludes or sees a risk and can't order release. And that causes great embarrassment and ideally if somebody spots it in time, we have another representative as a sort of a parrot. He can give no real assistance to the panel (judge).

---

52. In the event, this Governor 5 turned to be an effective advocate who saw her role, contrary to the guidance mentioned above, fully to engage with the examination of the evidence and to take the Secretary of State's line in detailed cross-examination, especially of the prisoner.

For the prisoner it can be confusing:

> When the lifer governor, I've forgotten his name, we got on quite well, you know chats and that, and when he sat there and said he was representing the Home Secretary, I thought, What?! What are you doing? I thought it seemed really strange to me, I don't know, he's representing the prison (a prisoner).

Even when the lifer governor is in agreement with the formal view, he may still find himself in a difficult position:

> Counsel: That is our evidence. I don't know if Mr (the lifer governor) wants to add anything?
> Lifer governor: I'm in an invidious position. I'm happy to support what has been said here as lifer governor, but I'm here as the Secretary of State's representative.
> Judge: So you'll stick to reading out his view. Yes, I think that is certainly the safest position.

The role of the legal representative

The legal representative was there to represent and to support. As one put it:

> (My role) is first of all to find out what the client wants to get out of the hearing, and then to advise them of what is possible and it's a sort of marrying exercise, I think between the aspirations on one side and the possibilities on another.. It's a process of interpretation as well as explaining to people what's going on. And there's a muscle element in it as well. Because they are on their own... And then there's the actual presentation of the case, the advocacy, which I think is actually the helping voice for someone (legal representative).

From a prisoner's perspective, a 'helping voice' was very necessary:

> I found it very very difficult, very very difficult at times. When I was talking to them and they asked me questions and I thought, what am I saying, what am I saying and I couldn't stop. I'm the kind of person that once I start talking I just keep on and I tend to just keep on and you'll get to where you're getting to. For some reason it wasn't working for me, I just wasn't getting to where I wanted to go and obviously they needed to ask the question again so having my brief there he was able to perhaps explain or put the question again (prisoner).

Eight prisoners were represented by counsel (of whom only one was a recall case). The main impact of certain counsel seemed to be to irritate the panel:

[The worst are] the loquacious, over intellectual and over philosophical (judge).

Have we got Miss X? I'm going home! (psychiatrist).

The skill of a good barrister could keep the panel firmly on their toes. However, perhaps the most influential lawyers were those who contributed least to the proceedings: who let their clients do the talking[53]. Occasionally a legal representative made an impact inadvertently: one solicitor called the circuit judge chairman 'My Lord' throughout the hearing, drawing from the judge the comment at the end: 'There's no need, I'm only a circuit judge. But I quite like it!' The solicitor's 'naiveté' endeared her to the panel.

If the legal representative pushed too far, then he or she could turn the panel against their client, asking for release from a closed prison or for an early review when there was no obvious reason for it. In one case, it appeared to us that the legal representative was not acting under instructions, but simply disadvantaged his client by pushing too far.

Panels, on the other hand, were grateful to legal representatives who had managed to persuade their clients to have more modest or 'reasonable' expectations:

I am very glad that the solicitor has taken the realistic view and persuaded him (judge).

There is no doubt in our minds, or in the minds of those we interviewed, that a good and sympathetic legal representative facilitates and improves the panel's decision-making.

The importance of experience among legal representatives

A legal representative who had carried out few DLPs was likely to be surprised by the informality, and the lack of procedural rigidity. They were less aware of the risk factors which were the panels' concern. It was helpful 'if they knew the drill', as a judge commented. Experience was important as was a talent for letting the prisoner's own voice come through. Some of the more experienced legal representatives ran the risk of speaking

---

53. This is linked to a concern that the more articulate prisoners may be more likely to succeed in achieving their aim for the hearing.

instead of the prisoner. Effective legal representatives were competent, realistic and knew their clients well. Barristers were a 'mixed blessing': the requisite skills were not in cross-examination, but were marrying the prisoner's expectations with the primarily inquisitorial process before them. Legal representatives had to present the best case, or allow the prisoner to present the best case, and needed sufficient knowledge of the prisoner, the process and the purposes of the panel, to achieve this. They were the legal equivalent of a good home probation officer: those with good relationships with their clients contributed positively to the prisoner's progress.

Reflecting on themes

So far in this chapter, we have considered the role of the individual participants in the DLP process. In this next part, we draw out certain themes, which allow us to move towards our conclusions. Whilst we found unanimous support for the concept of an oral hearing, the balance of advantage over disadvantage is more complex and can only be explored by returning to first principles: the aims of the discretionary lifer panel and the appropriate terms of reference.

The importance of the oral hearing

> This is a case where the DLP process works. By seeing him it's taken away my concerns (independent member).

> None of us were really in favour of that young man before the hearing, though I wasn't sure (independent member).

We found almost universal support for the oral hearing, that is, the presence of the prisoner, except for a few respondents who felt that the small number of cases where no positive recommendations were made at all, or where all recommendations were for release did not strictly require an oral hearing (on cost grounds). The decisions were clearly influenced by the oral part of the hearing. Panel members were either confirmed in their initial views, or they were assured that a move was justifiable, despite their initial reservations. There were several reasons why oral hearings were important:

- information in the dossier could give a one-sided picture of the prisoner and his or her level of risk

- legal representatives could in some cases facilitate a positive presentation by the prisoner and make a strong case for release or transfer.l
- prisoners were generally satisfied that an oral hearing was a fair and open process, compared with decisions made on paper. Oral hearings showed that each case 'was taken seriously' and that their view was heard
- risk assessments are 'human judgements'
- oral hearings (even where a decision was fairly clear) gave panels the opportunity to communicate directly to a prisoner in a formal setting about what was required in order to obtain release: ('say that to yourself every day', counselled one judge).

They were fraught occasions for prisoners, and inevitably, some felt disadvantaged because they 'said the wrong thing', became inarticulate, or did not present well:

The last one, I knew I'd 'failed' the oral hearing, that I'd failed on the oral. You think, 'what did I say that was wrong?'

You feel very vulnerable...

I spent one and a half hours answering questions abut my sexuality. Then got a two year knock-back as a result.

Having an oral hearing inevitably meant that appearance or presentation influenced the panel, and this could operate both to the prisoner's advantage and to their disadvantage[54]. Sometimes legal representatives participated too much and came between the panel and a prisoner, who might end up saying very little.

We noted earlier how the bureaucratic constraints of the oral hearing process led to delays: whilst a prisoner is entitled to a hearing every two years, this was not always achieved. We are also conscious that the prospect of a forthcoming DLP could slow down a prisoner's progress through the prison system. We return now to the objectives of the DLP process.

The objectives of the DLP process

Participants agreed that the main object was for the panel to decide if it was safe to release someone, and if not whether some other recommendation should be made. Although the

---

54. We have no way of knowing how panels would have decided the cases we observed had there not been an oral hearing. This is an area for further research.

decision is made by the Parole Board, this is not an ordinary 'parole' or early release decision, where rehabilitative aims may be clearer, and where the prisoner is going to be released in any case in a relatively short time[55]. In DLP cases, the prisoner has already served the tariff specified by the sentencing judge: (s)he is having time 'added', rather than time 'deducted' from his/her sentence. The object of the hearing was to give the prisoner an opportunity to present his/her case, and for the panel to test the evidence. There was widespread disagreement whether the process should have other objectives of a steering or therapeutic nature: some Prison Service staff also suggested that the process had a subsidiary role as an independent check on the use of authority over prisoners. However, this was not the 'main' objective. Participants acknowledged that the hearing might have different objectives from the prisoner's perspective.

For the purposes of this discussion, we consulted Elizabeth Barnard's five main objectives of parole: rehabilitation, reward, management tool, cost saving and public protection[56]. But these five objectives may be given different emphasis in relation to discretionary lifers, and at different times, or by different decision-makers.

Reward and cost-saving reflect the 'penological pragmatism' often held to underpin the operation of parole procedures at a general level. Rehabilitation and to some extent, public protection, can be regarded as more traditional aims relating to the individual. Public protection now has embedded within it the modern managerialist (or actuarial) risk prediction paradigm: the assumption that degrees of risk of reoffending can be measured and predicted, in addition to the requirement for supervision identified by Barnard. Most of the people we spoke to thought the key objective of a panel hearing was to assess risk, to see whether the prisoner could be released without exposing the public to unacceptable risk.

But there was an acknowledgement that there were other objectives too: giving the prisoner a voice; fully and independently reviewing the case; in some cases, 'a chance to right a few

---

55. In determinate cases, the Parole Board has regard to the protection of the public and 'the desirability of preventing the commission by them of further offences and of securing their rehabilitation' (s32(6) of the Criminal Justice Act 1991). For a review of parole decision-making, see Hood and Shute, 1995 and Hood and Shute, 2000.
56. In her more detailed account, they are:
   - the long-term *rehabilitation* of the prisoner. ... Traditionally, this has been the dominant official goal, particularly at the introduction of parole
   - to modify the sentence of the court in the light of later behaviour, as a reward to the prisoner. This has been played down in official policy but has been seen as influencing decisions
   - to give correctional agencies more control over their work, by affecting the population of prisons and providing an incentive to good behaviour. In this respect parole is a management tool
   - to reduce public *expenditure* as keeping people in custody is considerably more expensive than other measures
   - for public *protection*, by providing controls over ex-prisoners, rather than discharging them without supervision (Barnard, 1976: 153, paraphrased).

wrongs' (psychiatrist); and a check on the treatment and management of lifers, even though these other objectives were infrequently expressed in the language of rights:

> [Its main purpose?] An independent check upon our use of authority as a whole and the power that the Prison Service and by virtue of that the secretary of state has over the prisoner (lifer governor).

> People who are sentenced to an indeterminate sentence, I think, do need a degree of reassurance that their case is being looked at and is not forgotten, or lost in some bureaucratic maze (independent).

There was, however, little concern expressed about the post-tariff status of prisoners.

The assessment of risk had to be carried out in a fair and objective manner, in the interests of prisoners' (human) rights. There was considerable disagreement as to whether, having considered a case, the panel should be 'putting down markers for LMU' or be 'giving them a shopping list of things they've got to do' (legal representative). Some panel members (and lifer governors) felt that a hearing could (re)motivate a prisoner, 'give them a kick-start just after' so they think 'oh well I'd better get me head down and get some offending behaviour done':

> I've been on a panel, when this chap has been about 26 years in prison in a Cat B establishment, he did not want to come up or participate or co-operate with the parole process; anyway the panel went down and asked him to come up, he did and they said., 'Fair enough you don't want to say anything about parole, but do you want to say anything to us?' He talked for an hour, and in the next few days we had a letter addressed to the panel saying, 'This man has changed, he's motivated'... If a chap is 18, 19, 20 years in that sort of confinement, and if he thinks somebody is listening to him it could act as a motivation, and they have a goal, they have something to work for... (panel secretary).

So panels (and others) saw the hearing as having a steering effect: reports get written, progress is considered and suggestions are made for future work. This was particularly so in higher security conditions, where release was not an option. Prisoners even argued that the hearings in high security prisons acted as a 'rehearsal' opportunity for later ones, where the stakes were arguably higher. Despite some reservations about the purpose of DLPs where release or transfer were not sought (expressed by one or two), most felt that panels conducted these hearings with the same degree of seriousness and thoroughness as any other:

...(H)e was allowed to talk about the way he'd changed, the progress he'd made, why he thought he was ready to move on and he was listened to with respect, and he was asked quite penetrating questions, but at least in a spirit of enquiry and not in a disparaging way. And he came out, and he was no nearer release when he came out...and he said, 'that was really good'. At least he's had his go (legal representative)[57].

Outcomes did matter too, of course, and prisoners who got 'knock-backs' could be demotivated and disillusioned. There were risks of expectations being raised and dashed. There were also difficulties with prisoners receiving clear signals from the panel about what they were recommending, and then the Prison Service taking a different course, 'and then the prisoners get really confused' (psychologist). The steering effect did not have any statutory status. Some felt that the Parole Board should stick very strictly to their statutory role:

The main function of a DLP is to assess the risk of certain categories of prisoners. (Anything else) is the wrong understanding of our role. We are not there to advise, or tell the Prison Service how to run their show (judge).

There were tensions between the Parole Board and Lifer Management Unit about movements through the system. Occasionally the Parole Board wanted to recommend transfer to open conditions from a Category B prison. They were satisfied that the prisoner no longer posed an unacceptable risk and was ready for 'testing' in open conditions. Their hands were tied by 'rules of thumb' requiring prisoners to move through the categories one at a time[58]. Many respondents saw the panel as independently reviewing Prison Service assessments and reports, 'sifting the facts', to counter any possible bias, weakness or oversight:

The objectives are to consider the risk that would be presented by releasing prisoners and to give the fullest opportunity for everything relevant to the decision to be placed before the panel. That's why I think the DLP process scores over other sorts of panels in that there are usually very few stones left unturned, because if we haven't found them, then the prisoner's legal representative is likely to draw attention to them (independent).

---

57. See Tyler (1990) for a discussion of the relationship between legitimacy and compliance; and the importance of process in perceptions of fairness.
58. The Lifer Manual (PSO 4700) says simply (at para 4.1): 'A typical male lifer will generally go through the following stages of the sentence prior to release on licence: local prison, Lifer Main Centre, Category B training or dispersal prison, Category C prison, Category D (open) prison, Resettlement facility (e.g. pre-release employment scheme (PRES)). While no two life sentences will be identical, exceptions to this general pattern will be rare'. The relationship between categorisation and risk needs further clarification.

Several respondents remarked that 'there is nothing that compares to it, in terms of the rigour of the process and the potential for a very detailed exercise of risk assessment so that a valuable opportunity would be lost if panels could not make recommendations that informed the management of the prisoner's sentence.

So although there was a clear consensus on the main issue (a fair and open process of risk assessment in order to review or justify continuing custody), there were different views about the scope of the objectives in practice and whether they were limited or could be broadened in practice. Legal representatives often put pressure on panels to make other recommendations, but most panels were generally keen to take on this role anyway and, at the very least, to reinforce positive recommendations made in reports. They wanted to 'do good' where good could be done, in often very difficult cases.

These quasi-rehabilitative and judicial objectives took on a different tone if the primary task was 'to protect the public'. In this case, risk assessment must necessarily be carried out cautiously and weighted in favour of public protection. The aim was not just to get the process right (that is, to be fair, and to move prisoners towards their release) but to get the right outcome: to avoid serious reoffending by released lifers. This placed major constraints on the panel, which we will discuss below. There were tensions between the need to be cautious and the need to be fair.

The terms of reference

Almost all our respondents raised the question of the terms of reference of the panel, which are to be found in the referral letter at the front of each dossier. Most felt that these terms of reference could be 'slightly widened' so that 'recommendations about what happened next' were formally allowed. But there were also strong feelings that 'this should be done elsewhere', that the Parole Board were effectively plugging a gap:

[by] 'formally taking on that role, it's letting other parts of the system off the hook, and it's not to the prisoners' advantage (psychiatrist).

Prisoners saw the panel as 'independent and powerful' in the face of 'a system that is failing them' and they (and their legal representatives) wanted pressure to be exerted on their behalf. Panel members were torn on this issue:

I'd love to (make recommendations about next steps) because that's so much part of the other work that I do, really thinking about what would be the best way forward for somebody to move. But I also recognise that just on one short interview and on papers I think it probably isn't right that we make recommendations... (psychiatrist).

Certain panel members felt strongly that their terms of reference should be broadened. In particular, several psychiatrists were keen to think of ways to help move prisoners forward, perhaps because this is what they do in their professional lives. They were conscious that prisoners can get 'stuck' in the system. This argument for making helpful recommendations was strongly supported by some judges and independents, though they were not asking to be able to direct such matters. Panel members were aware that they should not step outside their terms of reference, but there was a feeling that they should speak out when it was 'right to do so':

We widely ignore the guidance, I certainly do. If we think the chap is a Cat B and he should be a Cat C, I know we aren't supposed to say so, but we do. And if we think that certain things ought to be done, for example, he should be transferred to a mental hospital or something, you say so. Although these are not strictly part of our terms of reference, they can't stop us (judge).

I think if we are really worried, that there is something in a particular case in question, which calls for comment, then we will comment regardless of our terms of reference. I think we are sufficiently robust to go beyond our terms of reference if we need to (judge).

They felt as if they were nudging the process, nudging the Prison Service or the management of the prisoner. Or as one panel secretary said,

The evidence sort of drags you into saying something like that.

Despite this, there was a widespread appreciation of the fact the Prison Service was there to manage prisoners, and that the Parole Board should not encroach on territory which is rightly not theirs:

We would need to know an awful lot more about the prisons themselves, what they had to offer and we would need to have a much more hands on knowledge of the prisoner himself, throughout his prison sentence, before we could indulge in re-categorisation (judge).

Most panel members felt that making carefully considered and informed recommendations was appropriate, but that giving those recommendations statutory authority was inappropriate. There were difficulties with panel members assuming knowledge of individual prisons, the courses they had on offer and eligibility for them, but general recommendations (for example for a progressive move) were less controversial:

> They are making an observation...they're not directing and they say that in their letter. We are...looking at it with a fresh view, we have not the sort of tunnel vision ... Sometimes the psychiatrist on the panel thinks this man should be looked at by an independent psychiatrist, with a view to a transfer to a special hospital. The panel's observations have been taken into account, and as a result the man has been transferred to a hospital. I've seen that very often (HEO).

> The one I am about to do is not about releasing...The only business I've got and I do see it as an important one...is there a crumb that we can put into this process if you like, to start making him do some more work... It's unrealistic to think you've got a magic wand, but if there's two or three things we can do to say, 'if you start thinking about this for the future, you may be able to be a step further towards release'...so it's pretty small fry in one sense, yet it's pretty important (independent).

The main argument in favour of such recommendations was the amount of work involved and the generally high standard to which panel roles were performed. After considerable deliberation, the panel came to 'a considered view on the facts' (legal representative). They could also recommend early reviews, and this was a useful (but some argued, under-used) way in which the panel could influence the prisoner's movement:

> If the Parole Board...thinks that somebody is on the cusp of release, but they're just... either they need a few more home leaves or there's something that needs to be tested or if they want to give them a bit longer alcohol free or drug free...the Board ought to have the power to say, 'another review in twelve months' and the Home Office have to accept it rather than (override it) (legal representative).

There was considerable support for extending the terms of reference in relation to early reviews: several people suggested that such recommendations should be binding. However, the Prison Service was nervous that an early review might be recommended simply 'to give the prisoner something'. The current position, where recommendations were not formally sanctioned and had no formal or legal power, but were frequently made and often influenced subsequent events, was confusing, but seemed to achieve a compromise most people could live with. We would wish to see this part of the panel's role strengthened, particularly whilst the movement of life sentence prisoners through the system is slow and haphazard (see Chapter Six). Training on how to make general recommendations helpfully might reduce tension between the panels and both LMU and LRU.

Prisoners were well aware that they might have a more 'sympathetic' hearing from panels than from the Prison Service and would like to see the Parole Board play a more active part all through their sentence planning, largely because of their independence of the prison authorities. They would increase the powers of the Parole Board to direct open and progressive moves (although not to direct them to complete more and specified courses), largely because they have more faith in the Parole Board than in the Prison Service to act fairly and in their favour.

Panel members commented that the Prison Service was 'too touchy' on such matters. Tied to this was an awareness that if the DLP recommends something which the Prison Service did not accept, the prisoner was likely to be doubly disappointed. Control, whilst apparently in the hands of the panel, was in reality in the hands of lifer liaison officers or Prison Service headquarters. It was also clear that individual panel members would have liked more feed-back about whether their recommendations were being accepted (although the Parole Board is sent a copy of the letter to the prisoner in response to DLP recommendations).

There was a tension or frustration here: many people told us that they were aware that the DLP did not have the whole picture and should not be able to direct changes to classification etc., but at the same time a lot of careful consideration had gone into the decision-making process. Both judges and legal representatives suggested that at the least someone from LRU or LMU should have to come and report back personally to the Parole Board on why the recommendation was not being accepted:

> It makes more work for them, but that's what they're there for. It is a useful service we give ministers. Here is an independent body, judging a mass of evidence, and we think, in our view that this guy should actually be decategorised. Now if you think differently that's fine, but you've got to give the guy reasons for that. And I don't see anything wrong with that (Parole Board).

Some of those who felt that it was appropriate that panels should not make recommendations also argued that their limited powers should be more widely known in order to save time wasted on oral hearings for prisoners who were not seeking release or transfer to open conditions.

Perhaps unsurprisingly, some Prison Service staff felt that DLPs should have no powers of recommendation: it caused too much confusion and was better left to 'case management'. The argument was that legal representatives were using DLPs to by-pass normal categorisation procedures, which involved the police, etc. But this was not unanimous. One LLO suggested that a High Court judge should be incandescent that a civil servant has the right to overturn his recommendations. And another commented:

> I think it is appropriate to make some sort of comment on how close you are or how far away. .. certainly in terms of giving the prisoners an appreciation of how much further they've got to go in their sentence, that's something very useful to them. It's also helpful as a manager to know what we should be pressing for operationally in terms of the courses for that prisoner as well (LLO, Cat A).

Several people commented to us on the seemingly illogical fact that panels could direct release, but merely recommend seemingly less important decisions:

> I think it's illogical that the panel should have the right to order release but only to recommend a move to Category D and not to make any recommendations other than that.. If we regard panels as having the expertise to decide release, then they should have the expertise to recommend a move from B to C. I would not be worried by that. The effect will be that men will progress through the system quicker, and more will be released. I think if that's the case it's incumbent on us to sharpen up our assessments. I wouldn't be worried by an increase in the power of the panel (psychologist).

Proposed solutions to this 'illogicality' varied, and many thought that it was an illogicality they could happily live with: it simply represented the law. Panels followed their terms of reference, but also wandered beyond them. There was clearly a tension between the requirements of the Prison Service for the flexible management of potentially dangerous prisoners, and the role of the Parole Board[59].

---

59. A paper by Jones and Creighton was circulated to the DLP Users group at its meeting in July 1999 which argued that the status of some recommendations should be raised to directive powers (particularly on moves to open conditions and the timing of future reviews). It also encouraged the Parole Board to consider adopting a 'wider' approach to recommendations relating to treatment such as commenting on the areas of risk which still need to be addressed and on possible places of treatment. We endorse their conclusion that where comprehensive risk assessments have been prepared by experts on both sides and where serious comment can be made about developments since the last hearing, panels should be enabled to comment freely in order to avoid increasing the risk of prolonging incarceration. We are glad to note that the Parole Board is developing a standard form of words to be used.

Parole Board Statement of Purpose

We look next at whether panels meet the standards suggested by the Parole Board Statement of Purpose:

> The Parole Board for England and Wales exists to carry out risk assessments to inform decisions on the early release of prisoners with the ultimate aim of protecting the public. We aim to be fair, open and consistent in all our decisions and to operate effective and efficient processes in order to consider cases in a timely manner.

We were impressed to learn that most respondents rated the process highly. When asked to quantify their judgement, most participants gave the process seven or eight out of ten; prisoners gave it less:

> I don't think it's very good – probably five. Everybody's trying to be nice without trying to upset anybody. It's a bit like going to see the headmaster (prisoner).

Our own view, formed over the life of the project, is that if a narrow version of the process is taken, then it is a reasonably fair process. As we will argue later, when seen in its full context, it seems less fair. Procedurally, it is very fair, but substantively it is less so. We shall return to this argument in Chapter Six.

Perceptions of fairness

The overwhelming feeling of panel members was that the process was fair, especially when compared with alternative processes. It was seen to be fair both to the prisoner and to the public, though some questioned whether the process of recall to prison was always fair.

Some legal representatives felt that the burden of proof should be reconsidered: was it fair that someone who was post-tariff had to prove that they were safe to be released, or should the Prison Service have to prove that it was necessary to detain them? A psychologist pointed out that he felt it was unfair when panels 'grilled' prisoners during a hearing: the panel was not the right context in which to conduct an in-depth interview. Some prisoners thought that it was unfair that the Secretary of State, who had never met the prisoner, should be allowed a view, let alone a veto. There was also some concern that prisoners and panels did not have all the information held by Prison Service (for example, adjudication records, or Security Information Reports). Some prisoners felt that the informality was unfair. One, for example, complained that he did not like sitting round a table with all the witnesses sitting in throughout.

Recall hearings were regarded as less fair, particularly because of the delays involved.

Perceptions of openness

Our questions on openness were interpreted partly as questions on disclosure. Although the Prison Service had information on prisoners which was not disclosed, all participants felt that the system of disclosure for DLPs worked well. In all but a tiny minority of cases, where the chairman may direct that a document should be withheld, prisoners see all that the panel sees. Although the Rules provide that information may be withheld from the prisoner on the grounds that its disclosure would 'adversely affect' his or other people's health or welfare, this did not occur in our study. Lawyers were rightly concerned by the rule that such information should be served on the prisoner's representative, since a lawyer who knows more than his or her client is in an invidious (and unprofessional?) position.

Openness came at a price:

> Some psychologists feel it's too open, if he's a dangerous man and the psychologist is closely associated with the decision not to release him.. certainly I've had death threats and threats on the panel. The last one I did the guy shouted at me 'You're a fucking slag, I hope you fucking die of fucking cancer'. That's an inevitable consequence of it being open (psychologist).

Prisoners and prison staff wondered why they could not have been present for the deliberation:

> I would like to be more privy to their discussions, thoughts and impressions during and after the hearing. Then you can either agree or disagree with them and say why you felt you disagreed (prisoner).

Whilst most participants did not share that view, there was a common feeling (amongst lawyers, prisoners, prison staff) that letters could have been more detailed, more open in terms of explaining the reasoning which lay behind the panel's decision. No one wanted panels to have more publicity or media attention.

Perceptions of consistency

The DLP procedure was felt to be largely consistent, though with many minor deviations. Most participants were more concerned whether there was consistency in how the evidence was assessed, in decision-making. Some lawyers were sceptical about whether the panels were consistent in their decision-making, given that the panel seemed to be inconsistent in what evidence they wanted to hear and which witnesses they wanted to hear from.

Many panel members were reluctant to talk in terms of consistency: every case was different, and consistency was only a qualified good:

> I wouldn't like to see it more (consistent)...You would only ever be able to go on measurables and you would never be able to go on how somebody presented on the day (psychiatrist).

Recall hearings were perceived as the least consistent[60]. In July 1999 the DLP Users Group were circulated with a paper from LRU on inconsistent procedures at recalls. It was withdrawn at the request of the Chairman of the Parole Board to be dealt with subsequently between LRU and the Parole Board. In the paper, the LRU member who had presented the case at two recent recall hearings (one of which was in our study) complained that at one recall the panel had come across as being entirely neutral and even-handed in their approach, whilst at the other, it 'could not have been more different... the impression given was that the Prison Service were the opposition, with the judge, for example, asking the prisoner's solicitor how he wanted the proceedings to be conducted'.

Panel members were unaware of the procedures at other panels, and regularly asked us how theirs had compared with others (some commenting that they had never thought about this before). One or two panel members suggested good practice guidelines; and we were aware as we finished our research that this was in hand.

Perceptions of effectiveness

Most panel members felt that their effectiveness should be measured against their limited terms of reference: the success or otherwise of the decisions they made. We felt there were two key ways of looking at effectiveness: the quality of their decision-making; and the

---

60. In terms of outcome they were consistent: all the recalls in our study were confirmed. The procedures and the weighing of the evidence were perceived as inconsistent.

outcomes achieved. The quality of decision-making was good, though cautious. Their effectiveness in this respect was limited by the presence of the Secretary of State and the Lifer Review Unit 'over their shoulders'. A certain inertia was perceived in prisons, and the Parole Board was regarded with ambivalence if they challenged some of this inert practice. As a process, the panel hearings were good enough, and their decision-making careful enough, that we would wish to see them having more influence, with their recommendations trusted. We consider their independence below.

The DLP process was only as effective as all the participants allowed it to be: the Parole Board was a small cog in the wider criminal justice system. Some legal representatives suggested that panels were becoming less effective: panels had been braver, encouraging some prisoners to jump from Cat B to Cat D, but they had now adopted the 'tramline' thinking of the Prison Service. On the other hand, some panel members felt that their effectiveness was sometimes limited by poor legal representation.

From the prisoner's point of view, a DLP was only effective if it moved them on.

Perceptions of independence

> How independent? Very. Oh very. The panel jealously guards its independence. I dislike the fact that the Parole Board is in the same building as the Prison Service. I think it gives a wrong message to the public, suggesting we are part of the Prison Service and we are not. We are wholly independent. We don't care tuppence what the Secretary of State's views are, really. We act independently of that. We rely on the Prison Service for their knowledge of the prisoner, and that's what we base our assessment on. But what the Secretary of State's views are…It is a factor but not one on which we should necessarily put too much weight (judge).

> You won't find many judges who will be leant on by Home Secretaries, or anyone else… Right or wrong, we're not pushed around (judge).

Judges did indeed 'fiercely guard' their independence, and one or two took some pleasure in contradicting the Secretary of State. Prisoners too were conscious of the independence of the Board:

> We're fairer, we're safer in the hands of a judge than a politician. He's less likely to be swayed by current trends and having to please a bigger master (prisoner).

Panels were made up of 'strong minded people', and the Parole Board was seen as having a 'strong leader'[61]. Prisoners perceived the Parole Board as acting independently during the hearing, but as constrained in their decision-making. They recognised that the independence of the Parole Board was limited since the Prison Service (or the Home Secretary) could veto recommendations.

Several panel members pointed out guidelines and directions from the Secretary of State (or from civil servants acting on behalf of the Home Secretary), whilst proudly indicating their resistance. Most interviewees assumed that panels were independent, and all argued that the DLP process provided 'an independent review' of the prisoner's case. As individuals, and as panels of the Parole Board, DLPs seek to act in total independence of the Prison Service: 'they don't bring any baggage with them (lifer liaison officer).

> If the Board isn't independent and doesn't robustly defend its independence, the members might as well be civil servants or something (Executive Officer).

This independence was, however, in some senses illusory. There were 'unhealthy feelings about the sort of cross-fertilisation between the lifer unit and the Parole Board' (legal representative). The following were given as examples of 'compromised independence': Parole Board members are appointed by the Home Secretary, psychiatrists who worked in (or who had worked in) prisons were used on the Board, the Parole Board is housed within the Prison Service and funded out of the Prison Service budget and many of the secretariat staff are seconded from the Prison Service. Whether the performance of the Parole Board would be made more effective by greater independence is uncertain: the greatest limitation on effectiveness seems to be the flow of information from the Prison Service 'downstairs' to the Parole Board. They were relatively independent in the decision-making, but 'not in the gathering of information'. Strengthening independence by moving the Parole Board to its own independent building might reinforce these problems.

The Parole Board was regarded by Lifer Management Unit as 'fiercely independent in taking decisions', yet this independence was not necessarily respected: in 1998-9, five out of 39 recommendations for moves to open conditions were rejected by the Home Secretary (12.8%). So when the Board got the decision 'wrong', the decision was adjusted accordingly. Their influence was constrained by their limited powers. Prisoners were aware that there was a double loop: the prison would 'wait for the DLP to decide', then the Parole Board 'merely recommends' and the Prison Service could ignore their recommendations. If transfer to open conditions was the important precursor to release, the Prison Service were 'all powerful' in making that decision.

---

61. At the time of this study Baroness Usha Prashar was chairman of the Parole Board.

We observed and heard many examples of the pressures operating on panels to be cautious throughout the decision-making process. Potential public and political 'mistakes' were very much on their minds. When asked about what pressures they were under when making decisions, panel members were at pains to stress that whilst there may be political and media pressures, they were independent and able to resist them. However, it was also clear that they consciously shouldered the burden of 'taking the risk' if they released anyone, and this was a heavy responsibility. Other pressures were: cost; the need to be 'judicial review proof', a natural caution; and public opinion. Parole Board staff were conscious of a pressure ('a constant stream of grumbles') from LRU.

Whilst we were discussing independence, it was pointed out to us that the role of the Secretary of State's representative was also a compromise, as at least two lifer governors gave us examples of having to take a different line at the hearing to their actual view about the prisoner. Legal representatives were sometimes dispirited by the lack of independence shown by lifer governors:

> This lifer governor will stand and chat to you outside the hearing and say, well really `I think he's ready for release'. But they won't put it in reports because they know the Home Office won't like it.... I can think of at least two lifer governors where I've said to them, you ought to have the courage of your convictions and say so. And there's a further instance where you've got a more junior officer, where the lifer governor actually kicked him into line and made him re-write his report. That's nothing to do with the Parole Board and quite how you get round it I don't know. You need a more sort of liberal and open Home Office which is open to independence (laughs) (legal representative).

Perceptions of efficiency

Most of those we interviewed interpreted 'effectiveness' at first as cost effectiveness. Was the DLP process a cost-effective method of decision-making? Efficiency was measured in terms of cost and time. In terms of cost, many participants were keen to point out that the cost was a small price to pay (£1,286 per case) for a good risk assessment, which balances the rights of the public with the rights of the prisoner. The system can be costed, as can the demand on resources of prolonging detention, but it is not possible to 'cost' the value of minimising mistaken decisions to end (or to prolong) detention. Did the process provide value for money?

We would argue, based on our observations, that it does. As a decision-making process it is thorough, balanced and reasonably fair. There were some inefficiencies, but these were related to delays and deferrals rather than to the operation of the hearings.

There was concern that the effectiveness of the DLP might be affected by cost savings (for example if panels were to lose panel secretaries). Others felt that lack of money in the Prison Service (i.e. shortages of suitable courses, etc.) made the DLP process less effective. Efficiency might include reducing the size of the prison population to best effect:

> Given the amount of money which is spent on keeping them inside, it's actually a fairly insignificant amount of money, provided the end quality and the decision is right (Lifer Review Unit).

> The amount of money we actually spend for everything we do is a drop in the ocean of the Prison Service's overall expenditure. For the importance of the role that we have, it's a particular drop in the ocean, and the idea of taking it up from whatever it is, let's say two million, if it became three million it would still be a drop in the ocean. I do think we are being kept back by some of these economies (independent member).

The main inefficiency was seen to be the submission of late reports, though some participants also questioned the need for oral hearings in all cases. Some legal representatives thought that judges were inefficient at looking at cases and thinking about them adequately when making their pre-panel directions.

The cost of the system could be reduced by more timely submissions of dossiers, by reducing the number of deferments, by offering prisoners the option of a paper hearing (or video links), by cutting members' fees and by transferring prisoners to open conditions more swiftly. Whether this would reduce costs without increasing the rate of mistaken decisions is a different question. Releasing less cautiously might also save on the cost of accommodating prisoners (but at the potential cost of more offences and/or recalls).

The confidence of panels in decision-making

All panel members were either confident or reasonably confident in the decisions they made. Few seemed to have sleepless nights about the decisions they took (unlike some of the lifer liaison officers who appeared before them). This might have been a reflection on the characters of those appointed to the Parole Board: a certain robustness was necessary in those taking such important decisions. Many argued that the expertise they shared was in making decisions. However, panel members also acknowledged that risk assessment was not an exact science, and that caution was necessary:

> I worry more about under-sentencing than I do about over-sentencing, so I worry more about releasing someone than I do about locking them up (judge).

Panel members were concerned about those prisoners who could have been released and had not been, and frequently challenged those who relied on the recall rate as a measure of success or failure. Thus, whilst they felt confident about individual decisions, they were conscious of the difficulty in measuring success.

Summary

This last descriptive chapter has explored the roles played by participants in the DLP process and their perspectives (and some of our own) on aspects of the process. We were impressed with the conduct of the hearings and by the roles played by the three key members of the panel. Judges normally chaired proceedings well. Where they did not, other panel members were often able to intervene. Sometimes the panel hearings were chaired in an unfriendly manner. Psychiatrists and independent members had full and useful roles to play. The panel operated as a team, and we agreed that this was a useful method of decision-making. Panel secretaries were essential, but sometimes became over-involved (and at other times, too detached). Witnesses played an influential role when they were called, but this happened unsystematically. The role of the prisoner required some further thought: was the prisoner the 'key witness', defending himself or herself against the accusation of 'being risky', or should the burden of proof lie on the State? Panels were rightly discriminating about the reports they received and the expert witness advice they were offered. Home probation officers played a very important role, particularly in release cases, and were often required to attend a hearing before the panel were satisfied. The Secretary of State's role was confusing and often minimal. The legal representative could play a very useful role both to the panel and to the prisoner.

There was overwhelming support for the oral hearing, despite some risks relating to presentation. It was seen as a fair process, particularly if a narrow view of its main objectives was taken.

We found it difficult to draw conclusions about the quality and effectiveness of the decision-making process without returning to the objectives of the process. The main objectives of the hearings were very clear and all panels operated to this end (to decide whether it is 'no longer necessary' for the protection of the public that the prisoner should be confined). There were other important objectives, including the legal requirement to conduct a review. We felt that the process was sufficiently thorough, and that recommendations made outside their strict terms of reference should be treated seriously.

We consider our conclusions and the implications of them in our final chapter.

Part three
Conclusions and implications: putting the protection of the public first

"Perhaps the most sensitive area of public confidence is that of release of prisoners serving life sentences who have committed grave and violent offences" (Parole Board 1973: 28). In the following year there was a further reassuring statement that "the greatest care is taken in consideration of prisoners' cases for parole especially where a prisoner's previous offences show a record of violence...when an offender has shown himself to be dangerous his chances of parole may give rise to serious public anxiety, the Board's recommendations give first priority to the public interest." (Parole Board, 1973: 8) (in Coker and Martin, 1985: 37).

6   Conclusions and implications

Introduction[62]

This chapter moves from the descriptive to the analytic. We shall not attempt here to provide any detailed summary of the material in the preceding descriptive chapters – for that purpose, readers are directed to the factual summaries we have provided at the end of each chapter. Rather, in this concluding chapter we shall try to address the evaluative and policy implications of our work, with special reference to the seven questions posed to us by the Home Office at the outset of our inquiry.

Of those seven questions, two seem to us to be fundamental. They are, first, whether the DLP process can be considered fair, and secondly, how panels assess risk. We would argue, however, that these are anything but straightforward questions. We therefore begin this chapter by considering what we have come to regard as seven key conceptual issues that have been raised by our research – issues that, between them, are centrally relevant to the core questions of fairness and of the assessment of risk in the DLP process.

Seven key conceptual issues

Issue 1: The significance of a prisoner being 'post-tariff'

Our research has uncovered a strange paradox. DLPs were created in direct response to the judgement of the European Court of Human Rights in *Thynne*[63], and a central feature of that judgement was the 'post-tariff' status of the applicant discretionary life sentence prisoners. Article 5 of the ECHR provides a 'right to liberty'. In the analysis of the ECHR, once a prisoner moves beyond the tariff (or punitive element) part of his/her sentence, then he/she enters a different phase of custody. The prisoner is no longer being detained as a punishment for his/her offence(s), but solely for the protection of others. As such, he/she is entitled to special judicial protection. Extending this line of argument, one might say that the Parole Board, in dealing with DLP cases, is operating within a fundamentally different conceptual framework than it is when handling the rest of its caseload: instead of considering prisoners for a reduction in their 'normal' sentence (i.e. considering them for

---

62. This chapter is co-authored by Professor Anthony Bottoms (see Acknowledgements).
63. (1991) 13 EHRR 666.

'time off'), it is considering whether to detain them for longer than the normal sentence because of the risk that they pose (i.e. 'time added on' on the grounds of dangerousness). It is relevant to note, in this regard, that some scholars who have argued strongly for the ethical justifiability of special sentences for 'dangerous offenders' have nevertheless insisted that, in fairness to such prisoners, the special custodial status of people who are detained solely for the sake of others must always be recognised (see Walker, 1996).

By contrast to all this, most panel members whom we interviewed emphasised that the fact that a prisoner was post-tariff was irrelevant to the panel's assessment of his/her level of dangerousness, and hence to the panel's discharge of its central task, namely that of considering whether 'it is no longer necessary for the protection of the public that the prisoner should be confined' (s.28(6)(b) of the Crime (Sentences) Act 1997)[64]. They were, in our judgement, quite right in making this assessment, given the specific language of the statute.

Hence the paradox. DLPs were created in response to the ECHR recognition of the special status of 'post-tariff' lifers, but such special status plays almost no part in the thinking of DLPs as they discharge their central tasks. We shall consider below whether this apparent anomaly can be overcome, without altering the statutory test, yet without rendering nugatory the concept of a special 'post-tariff' status. To anticipate, we believe that it can, using the concept of competing rights.

Issue 2: Giving proper recognition to competing rights

With the incorporation of the European Convention of Human Rights into the domestic law of the UK, those concerned with legal and social matters in this country enter conceptual territory that is in important respects unfamiliar. The UK has an unwritten constitution (hence there are no entrenched constitutional rights, and a sovereign Parliament has had unchallenged power to repeal any right granted in previous legislation); domestic policy has been deeply influenced by the philosophical inheritance of utilitarianism, which is notoriously suspicious of the language of rights (Bentham roundly declared that to speak about fundamental rights is to talk 'nonsense on stilts').

UK. citizens have for long had access to the protection of the Convention through the European Commission and Court of Human Rights. But, until the very recent incorporation of the Convention into UK law, even a successful appeal by a British subject to the ECHR has had a limited impact upon UK law as a whole. Certainly, the UK government has had a duty under

---

64. See Appendix 1.

the Convention to remedy the adjudged breach of human rights – as it did after *Thynne* by enacting the special DLP legislation. But such remedial actions have been necessarily piecemeal, and they have not, by and large, altered the general character and context of UK law and policy, as described above. Hence, the post–Thynne DLP legislation was, on the ground and in practice, implemented by persons and institutions that might have only a partial understanding of the conceptual underpinnings of the jurisprudence of the ECHR.

One important aspect of this jurisprudence is the notion of competing rights. Citizens have rights, but these rights often cannot all be exercised in full without clashing with other rights (my general right to free speech would necessarily clash with your right to be protected from racial harassment, should I wish to make a speech inciting violence against members of your ethnic group). Exactly this situation applies in the field of protective sentences for offenders adjudged to be dangerous. Offenders are detained, beyond the tariff, in order to protect the rights of ordinary citizens who, it is believed, would be at serious risk if they were released. But, in deciding so to detain them, the State overrides what would otherwise be their right to be released from prison when they have served the term that their offences were deemed to have deserved. It seems clear that, within this conceptual framework, a person's right should only be overridden in this way if there are compelling reasons to do so; and even where it is decided that his/her right has to be overridden, the State nevertheless has a duty to protect his/her rights to the greatest extent possible without compromising the rights of the citizen whose claim of right has been given priority.

But how can one meaningfully 'protect the rights' of a citizen whose *prima facie* right has already been overridden? The answer lies in protecting their rights as far as possible: thus the life sentence prisoner is entitled to continued vigilance, so as to ensure at all times that it is indeed still necessary for the *prima facie* right to be overridden. We suggest that a normative framework of competing rights has the potential to resolve and overcome the paradox that we noted above. When panels are considering the statutory test, they are primarily (and rightly) concentrating on the rights of possible victims. They therefore, rightly, operate on the assumption that the post-tariff status of the prisoner is not very important. But the ECHR forced the creation of DLPs to provide a *judicial* (court-based) protection for offenders' rights at the post-tariff stage. Continued vigilance to ensure due consideration of the right to be released, together with due consideration for the protection of the public, constitute the *dual task* of the panel at a hearing.

We further suggest that such a framework goes a long way towards providing appropriate normative concepts with which one can appropriately consider the Home Office's central question to us as researchers, namely whether the DLP process can be considered fair. The concept of 'competing rights' is a good way to think about substantive fairness (and procedural fairness is in itself an insufficiently robust test of the fairness of the DLP process). Any true test of the substantive fairness of a hearing has to include questions *both* as to whether the public's right to protection has been properly considered *and* as to whether the prisoner's right to liberty has been properly considered.

It is not only fairness, but also *the way risk is assessed*, that is affected by this framework. Dworkin, operating within a framework of competing rights, famously argued that a person should only be detained against his will for preventative reasons if the 'danger he presents is vivid' (Dworkin, 1977), not whenever we calculate that it would probably reduce crime if we did detain him. Bottoms and Brownsword developed this idea of 'vivid danger':

> We suggest that it [the concept of vivid danger] has three main components: seriousness (what type and degree of injury is in contemplation?); temporality, which breaks down into frequency (over a given period, how many injurious acts are expected?) and immediacy (how soon is the next injurious act?); and certainty (how sure are we that this person has acted as predicted?). The certainty element is pivotal. If there is a very low score on the certainty factor, then whatever the danger it is certainly not vivid. However, as the score increases on the certainty element, the risk becomes increasingly vivid and we then have to look very carefully at the kind of danger threatened (Bottoms and Brownsword, 1983).

In 83 per cent of the cases we saw, the Parole Board concluded that the prisoner was sufficiently dangerous that their detention was necessary to protect the public. Whilst we can draw no conclusions of our own as to whether the prisoners we saw presented a 'vivid' danger, we would expect that the *level* of risk as well as its presence or absence should be considered. The 'vivid danger' test reminds us that both the degree and the type of risk are important: both the *seriousness* and the *certainty* of the risk must be assessed, as rigorously as possible. That is, high certainty of a minor offence is insufficient and very low certainty of a serious offence is insufficient, to constitute a substantial risk.

Issue 3: The Parole Board as court

As we have argued, the European Court of Human Rights held in *Thynne*[65] that post-tariff discretionary life sentence prisoners are, because of their fundamental human rights, entitled to have the lawfulness of their continued detention decided by a 'court' at reasonable intervals and to have the lawfulness of any re-detention determined by a 'court'. Although

---

65. (1991) 13 EHRR 666

the Court did not explain in detail why a 'court' was necessary, it is clear that this was their interpretation of the European Convention of Human Rights. One can speculate that the principal reason for this required judicial involvement flows from the constitutional advantages of the separation of powers; a prisoner has access to the courts as independent arbiters of his/her fundamental human rights. If this line of argument is correct, then both the independence and the judicial nature of the panel are vital.

Our research suggests that not all participants in the process regarded panels in this light. The Parole Board, when dealing with normal parole cases is not acting as a court, and it is particularly important therefore to underline this vital difference. It was, we felt, important for the panel to be chaired by a judge. Whilst there was no reason why many psychiatrists or independent members would not make excellent Chairmen (or conversely why some judges make poor Chairmen!), judges are used to chairing courts, dealing with witnesses, evidence and so on. Their presence is also vital symbolically, reinforcing the fact that the Parole Board in the DLP context is acting as a court. We comment later as to why this 'court' should not be adversarial.

Because the panel is sitting as a court it has the power to make decisions (about release). Other 'decisions' are currently only recommendations. Whilst this makes sense from an administrative point of view, it is important that the Parole Board acts as, and is regarded as, a 'court'. Recommendations made by the Parole Board should therefore give the prisoner a public law 'legitimate expectation'[66]. Unless the Prison Service rejects a DLP recommendation within a certain time and with written reasons, it should become binding, with the prisoner able to take the Prison Service to judicial review if the recommendation is not acted upon.

Issue 4: The relationship between the Parole Board (DLP) and the Prison and Probation Services

The Parole Board cannot direct release unless 'it is no longer necessary for the protection of the public that the prisoner should be confined[67]. Before a prisoner can be considered 'safe', he or she must have been tested. From a competing rights perspective, the Prison Service owes a post-tariff prisoner a *duty* to allow them to be tested wherever possible. This is part of their right to be released as soon as it is safe to do so: in other words, the delivery of justice to discretionary lifers depends on how life sentence prisoners are managed, reviewed and treated in prison as well as how DLPs operate when a case is referred to them.

66. This mirrors the recommendation of the Woolf Report that prisoners' 'contracts' "could provide a platform for an application for judicial review" (Woolf, 1991, para 12.123)
67. s28(6)(b) Crime (Sentences) Act 1997.

We were concerned by evidence that prisoners sometimes 'got stuck in the system'; that is, sometimes there was a breakdown in the relationship between the prisoner and his or her establishment, resulting in a negative spiral whereby progress ceased, reports became increasingly negative, and reviews became futile. Prisoners who 'get stuck' in this sense could be reviewed internally in more constructive ways. Similarly, we were concerned when it seemed that a prisoner stayed in prison simply because courses from which he would benefit were available in prison but not in the community, or stayed in prison because hospital beds were not available outside. We felt during our research that the provision of adequate support for released lifers in the community was patchy. Closer working between the Prison Service and the Probation Service may reduce this problem.

We were also concerned at not infrequent expressions of a paternalistic concern that 'we must not set them up to fail'. Obviously, external support should be as good as possible; but ultimately, if a prisoner is considered safe to be released, s/he has a right to be released, and paternalistic concerns should not hinder them.

Issue 5: Burdens of proof

It is inherently difficult for the prisoner to show that it is safe to release him. (How does a rapist 'prove' he will not reoffend?) The Crime (Sentences) Act 1997 specifies that the Parole Board should not direct release unless it is 'satisfied that it is no longer necessary for the protection of the public that the prisoner should be confined' (s28(6)(b)). Whilst this puts a clear burden on the Parole Board to be satisfied, it says nothing about whether there is either an evidential or a persuasive burden of proof sitting on one of the 'parties' to the hearing. It sometimes appeared that panels felt that the prisoner had a 'persuasive' burden. Yet some lawyers suggested, to the contrary, that the Home Secretary should have the burden of proving that the prisoner is not safe to be released. We became increasingly conscious that any discussion of a 'burden of proof' was both misleading and problematic.

Having established as we believe we have in Issue 2 above that the DLP has a dual function, we conclude that it should operate in this context with two legal presumptions:

- a safety presumption: they cannot release unless they are satisfied that 'it is no longer necessary for the protection of the public that the prisoner should be confined'. If in doubt, they do not release him

- a human rights presumption: post-tariff discretionary lifers must be released as soon as possible, and should be given every opportunity to be 'tested for safety'. They must be given priority to be released as soon as they are 'safe', which means they should have priority in recategorisation, courses, opportunities to work in the community, etc.

Issue 6: An inquisitorial or an adversarial process?

The essential difference between inquisitorial and adversarial procedures is whether the 'judges' or decision-makers are proactive. There was a tension pulling the DLP process in inquisitorial and adversarial directions simultaneously. It appeared that panels had originally been envisaged as 'inquisitorial' in the sense that it was assumed that they would play a major part in shaping the presentation of the evidence at the hearing, calling and questioning witnesses themselves, and so on; while the 'parties' would ask only supplementary questions. As time has passed, the process has become more adversarial, in the sense that panels leave the presentation of the case to the parties, who prepare their case, call, examine and cross-examine their witnesses. This has happened, we conclude, largely because judges and lawyers are more comfortable with their usual adversarial forum.

However, the panel must be proactive in this context. It is appointed for its expertise, for the balance that the panel itself reflects. For example, the psychiatrist member of the panel has the skills to ask searching questions which should not be left to the two 'adversarial sides'. We suggest that the panel should be consciously proactive in two senses:

- testing for risk/safety
- testing whether the Prison and Probation Services are respecting the prisoners' human rights.

By acknowledging this 'proactive role', the roles of the other parties can be clarified. Thus, for example, the Secretary of State's representative has a vital function, but he or she should not be forced to play an adversarial contest ('boxing match') with an opposing lawyer.

Issue 7: The status of 'risk factors' as indicators of risk

We have explored in Issue 2 above why, if competing rights are to be recognised, this must affect the way in which risk is assessed. The various factors or criteria which panels considered as they formed their decision about whether or not to release or transfer in each case were considered in Chapter Four. What we have not explored is to what extent the risk factors considered really are indicators of risk. It is beyond the scope of this study to evaluate the research evidence that these risk factors have robust predictive value, but it may be that some of the beliefs on which the decision-making process is based are unfounded. Some validated risk factors (such as age, experience of local authority care, number of convictions at an early age and so on) were not discussed during the decision-making process; others (the experience of violence and abuse, absence of a positive role model, disrupted educational history, susceptibility to peer pressure, low self-esteem, and so on) were considered haphazardly. Whether what panels did during a hearing could accurately be called 'risk assessment' without more standardised and validated techniques at their disposal was a question which troubled us throughout the research process.

Nor have we explored what Keith Hawkins (1983) refers to as the 'master code' or 'decision-frame' which informs discretionary choices. Without standardised risk assessment tools, there was a danger that *assumptions* could be mistaken for *assessments*. Decisions were made with no explicit structure, but with some implicit 'taken-for-granted' assumption (e.g. that drinking regularly several pints of Guinness constituted sufficiently risky behaviour). In other words, what structures of values and meanings shape decision-making? What ends are sought? What constitutes risk? What sort of people are regarded as risky? How are the 'relevant' factors related to outcomes? What 'frame of meaning' operates as panels accomplish a hearing? Possible 'master frames' may be moral, organisational and professional, or operational, and these may constitute ideological frameworks which emphasise some values (for example, rehabilitation, efficiency, 'covering oneself', etc.) over others (like fairness). Master frames are 'subtle, shifting and interacting things' and may change over time (Hawkins, 1983: 22). Sometimes such shifts (for example in perceptions of what is an acceptable risk) become institutionalised, for example, in a redefinition of what sorts of decisions panels are making and to what end. We have identified, we think, a shift towards increasing caution by the Parole Board in this – one of its most important and carefully carried out tasks. We witnessed only one or two individual panel members with a 'resettlement' decision-frame. For a body traditionally associated at least in part with rehabilitation, but ostensibly carrying out a distinct task here (and with a much greater emphasis on risk), this was a finding worthy of further discussion.

Summary

The DLP has two core functions: to protect the public and to protect the rights of post-tariff prisoners (see Thynne (*supra*),. DLPs were set up as a 'court', with this dual function. A court is part of the judicial arm of the state, independent both of the legislature and of the executive. *Decisions* of this 'court' are clearly binding. Its *recommendations* should also create a 'legitimate expectation' that they will be respected by the Prison Service (unless rejected within a fixed time-frame). This will make their recommendations judicially reviewable and strengthen their role as a court. Given the dual function of this 'court', it is appropriate that it takes a lead in the investigation of the questions it has to answer. There should be a presumption in favour of public protection, balanced by a presumption in favour of prompt release where release is safe. Risk factors should only be taken into account if there is reasonable evidence of their *presence* and of their *relationship with serious offending.*

Conclusions

So what conclusions can we draw about the quality of the process; what criteria should be used for evaluating the process and what is the relationship between the decision-making process and the outcomes of that process? Having analysed the conceptual issues it becomes clearer that whilst the decision-making process was of a generally high quality, panels were hampered by lack of structural clarity about the framework within which these decisions were being taken. We are conscious that any exclusive emphasis on the operation of the discretionary lifer panel process may cloud the larger question of the fairness of the substantive outcome. Writing at the time when the European Court of Human Rights decided in *Venables and Thompson*[68] that the Secretary of State's role in fixing the tariff of HMPs was inappropriate, we became increasingly aware of the Secretary of State's dominance in a procedure which was created to give an independent tribunal, the Parole Board, the duty to monitor the legality of post-tariff detention. Whilst the Parole Board may direct release, no prisoner in this study was released unless he[69] was in open conditions. When the Parole Board recommended a transfer to open conditions, the Secretary of State held the trump card and could veto (or delay) the transfer.

For prisoners, and indeed for all those involved, the DLP process was hugely significant, in both practical and symbolic ways. Yet it appeared to us that the key decisions were taken at the transfer stage (at all levels, not just to open conditions) and that the power to make these decisions rested firmly with the Prison Service and the Home Secretary. The power of the Parole Board to direct release was in practice seriously constrained by powers and inertias lying elsewhere, which could automatically hold up progress.

---

68. Judgements delivered 16 December 1999, 30 EHRR 121.
69. We observed no female cases in open conditions.

Turning to our research questions, if a narrow view of the process is taken, then the DLP process is fair. We felt that the quality of the decision-making process was high and that decisions were reached carefully and after thorough consideration of all the available information. Yet, when seen in its fuller context, the DLP system seemed less fair. The significance of a prisoner being post-tariff, and the dual task of the DLP, needed emphasising.

The question of effectiveness depends of course on the criteria used. On the terms of reference currently applied, decision-making seemed effective. Yet, judging the DLP as a 'court', it clearly has limited powers and limited effect. If the role of the DLP as 'court' were strengthened, perhaps the significant problems of late reports and delayed hearings would decrease.

Procedurally we concluded that DLPs acted consistently. Inconsistencies of style were observed, but these inconsistencies had little effect on the consistency of the decision-making process. In any case, consistency was rightly regarded as a qualified good. Generally speaking, panels made strenuous efforts to be user friendly. Too much of a departure from formality could be disarming and frustrating for the other participants. Individual panel members brought their professional expertise to the task: their effectiveness in performing this role was diminished when the procedure became too 'adversarial' rather than 'inquisitorial'.

One of the panel's key tasks is the assessment of risk, an extremely difficult task, particularly with this group of prisoners. The style of risk assessment was more clinical than actuarial[70], and seemed to us cautious. The 'vivid danger' test suggests the need to weigh both seriousness and certainty of risk, yet panels seemed to avoid discussing levels of risk. The 'master frames' are worth exploring further.

We voice a particular concern about the recall process. Whilst recall hearings were conducted similarly to ordinary DLPs, the issues raised were very different. In a recall case, the panel was being asked not only to assess risk, but to confirm the recall of someone who had previously been deemed safe to release. The reality of power seemed to lie with the Probation Service. The human rights implications of this are too easily ignored. The management of risk needs carefully distinguishing from the assessment of risk.

Do panel hearings represent value for money? Given the human rights obligations of the Parole Board, the relative expense of the process is justified. Resources are wasted in delays and deferrals, but if the positive duty on the Prison Service to move post-tariff prisoners swiftly towards release were acted on, this would save money.

---

70. As Hood and Shute also found (Hood and Shute, 2000).

We were aware, and many participants in our research mentioned it, of the implications for the conduct of DLPs of the increasing numbers (and different types of offenders) likely to enter the system as a result of the automatic life sentence, introduced by the Crime (Sentences) Act 1997. We end our report with the warning offered by one of our respondents:

> I think for the future, I do worry about the system's ability to allocate so much time, energy and expertise to DLPs, because the number of cases that are coming through, and the two strikes, three strikes, no strike, one strike discretionary lifers – because they are not to do with risk as I understand risk. It is to do with the public and the politicians…It's very difficult, it seems to me, to be working with those people to reduce the risk because…risk isn't that high to start with, so to put that sort of discretionary lifer in with the other lot of legitimate, if you like, discretionaries, and have the same process to do risk reduction…I think you're just mixing apples and oranges…So there will be all sorts of discretionary lifers and increasing numbers of them, and I just wonder how long before the DLPs become like MLPs, they get too many cases, and make the decisions with inadequate information.. (Parole Board).

Whilst Parliament seems in the 1997 Act to have tipped the scales in favour of protecting the public, it has also, in the Human Rights Act 1998, by implication, also emphasised the competing rights of the prisoner. A thorough understanding of the competing rights framework seems likely to be increasingly important in this area of policy.

Recommendations

- The significance of a prisoner being 'post-tariff' needs to be underlined.

- The DLP should be recognised as 'court-like' and perhaps renamed as a Parole Court for this purpose[71].

- Recommendations made by the Parole Board should, unless rejected by the Home Secretary within a fixed time-frame and with written reasons, create 'legitimate expectations' for prisoners which could be subject to judicial review.

- Since the DLP is a court, documents not produced in advance should not be admitted at the hearing.

---

71. Whether the Parole Board itself is correctly named is a separate question we raise here, given the changing framework of early release.

- Panels should separate the decision about risk (and the reasons for that) from the decision about directions or recommendations (and the reasons for that). This two-stage process would lead to more explicit decision-making, and greater consistency of approach.

- In recall cases, panels should separate the confirmation of the recall decision from the current risk assessment.

- There is a need for more training and procedural guidance. In particular, the empirical status of risk factors should be available to all participants in the process; panel secretaries and Secretary of State's representatives require guidance on role.

- There should be more formal feedback from the Prison Service on the outcome of recommendations and to the Prison Service on the quality and timeliness of reports.

- Further research on the effective management of life sentence prisoners (including their movement through categories) should be carried out.

Appendix 1:

Sections 28 and 32 of the Crime (Sentences) Act 1997

Duty to release certain life prisoners

Section 28.–

(1) A life prisoner is one to whom this section applies if –

(a) the conditions mentioned in subsection (2) below are fulfilled; or

(b) he was under 18 at the time when he committed the offence for which his sentence was imposed.

(2) The conditions referred to in subsection (1)(a) above are –

(a) that the prisoner's sentence was imposed for an offence the sentence for which is not fixed by law; and

(b) that the court by which he was sentenced for that offence ordered that this section should apply to him as soon as he had served a part of his sentence specified in the order.

(3) A part of a sentence specified in an order under subsection (2)(b) above shall be such part as the court considers appropriate taking into account –

(a) the seriousness of the offence, or the combination of the offence and other offences associated with it; and

(b) the effect of any direction which it would have given under section 9 above which section 67 of the Criminal Justice Act 1967 would have had if it had sentenced him to a term of imprisonment;

(c) the provisions of this section as compared with those of sections 33(2) and 35(1) of the 1991 Act.

(4) Where in the case of a life sentence prisoner to whom this section applies the conditions mentioned in subsection (2) above are not fulfilled, the Secretary of State shall direct that this section shall apply to him as soon as he has served a part of his sentence specified in the direction.

(5)   As soon as, in the case of a life sentence prisoner to whom this section applies –

    (a)   he has served the part of his sentence specified in the order or direction ('the relevant part'); and

    (b)   the Parole Board has directed his release under this section,

It shall be the duty of the Secretary of State to release him on licence.

(6)   The Parole Board shall not give a direction under subsection (5) above with respect to a life prisoner to whom this section applies unless –

    (a)   the Secretary of State has referred the prisoner's case to the Board; and

    (b)   the Board is satisfied that it is no longer necessary for the protection of the public that the prisoner should be confined.

(7)   A life prisoner to whom this section applies may require the Secretary of State to refer his case to the Parole Board at any time –

    (a)   after he has served the relevant part of his sentence; and

    (b)   where there has been a previous reference of his case to the Board, after the end of the period of two years beginning with the disposal of that reference; and

    (c)   where he is also serving a sentence of imprisonment or detention for a term, after the time when, but for his life sentence, he would be entitled to be released.

And in this subsection 'previous reference' means a reference under subsection (6) above or section 32(4) below.

(8)   In determining for the purpose of subsection (5) or (7) above whether a life prisoner to whom this section applies has served the relevant part of his sentence, no account shall be taken of any time during which he was unlawfully at large within the meaning of section 49 of the Prison Act 1952.

(9)   An offence is associated with another for the purposes of this section if it is so associated for the purposes of Part i of the 1991 Act.

Section 32.—

(1)   If recommended to do so by the Parole Board in the case of a life prisoner who has been released on licence under this Chapter, the Secretary of State may revoke his licence and recall him to prison.

(2)   The Secretary of State may revoke the licence of any life sentence prisoner and recall him to prison without a recommendation by the Parole Board, where it appears to him that it is expedient in the public interest to recall that person before such a recommendation is practicable.

(3)   A life prisoner recalled to prison under subsection (1) or (2) above –
      (a)   may make representations in writing with respect to his recall; and
      (b)   on his return to prison, shall be informed of the reasons for his recall and of his right to make representations.

(4)   The Secretary of State shall refer to the Parole Board –
      (a)   the case of a life prisoner recalled under subsection (1) above who makes representation under subsection (3) above; and
      (b)   the case of a life prisoner recalled under subsection (2) above.

(5)   Where on a reference under subsection (4) above the Parole Board –
      (a)   directs in the case of a life prisoner to whom section 28 above applies; or
      (b)   recommends in the case of any other life prisoner, his immediate release on licence under this Section, the Secretary of State shall give effect to the direction or recommendation.

6)   On the revocation of the licence of any life prisoner under this section, he shall be liable to be detained in pursuance of his sentence and, if at large, shall be deemed to be unlawfully at large.

Appendix 2: Index offence and time served of sample

Index offence

Twenty-seven per cent of the prisoners had been convicted of murder; 25 per cent of manslaughter; 17 per cent of arson; 13 per cent of rape; 6 per cent of other violent offences (including wounding with intent to murder and wounding with intent to cause grievous bodily harm) and 12 per cent of other sexual offences.

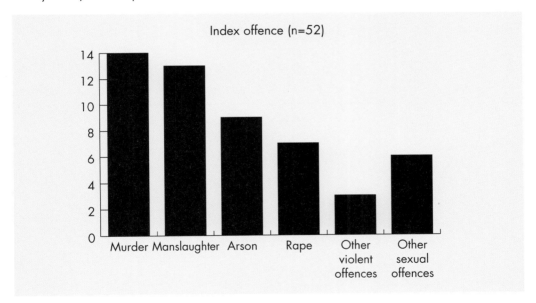

Index offence (n=52)

Time served

The average time served (at the time of the observed hearing) was 13 and a half years (including recalls), ranging from three years to 29 and a half years). The average length of tariff was eight years, with a range of two to 17 years. The average length of time served since tariff expiry was five years, with the longest time served since tariff expiry being 15 years and six months. The average number of months between recall and the first DLP was just over seven months, and for those whose subsequent hearings we observed, the average time served was five years six months (with a range from three years three months to nine years).

Nine of the prisoners in the sample had their first DLP oral hearing within one month of their tariff expiry.

	DLP	HMP	Recalls
Average time served	12 years 9 m	11 years 10 m	18 years 6 m
Range of time served	3 years to 29 years 6m	5.5 years to 19 years 1m	12 years 4m to 28 years 9m
Average tariff	7 years 5m	9 years 6m	10 years 3m
Average time since tariff	5 years 6m	2 years 3m	8 years 1m
Range of time since tariff	0 to 15 years 6m	0 to 7 years 1m	6 months to 13 years 9 m

Appendix 3: Interview questions and analytical guide for observations

Interview schedule

Introduction: we are mainly interested in the decision-making process – its quality and effectiveness. The questions we ask are general, but feel free to draw on examples and specific cases when you answer. [Record respondent details: role, number of hearings attended.]

1. On a scale of 1-10, how well do you think the DLP process works?

2. What are its main objectives?

3. What aspects of the process do you think work particularly well?

4. Which aspects work least well?

5. Are there any ways in which it could be improved?

6. What do you see as your main role in the process?

7. What is the role of the panel secretary?

8. How important do you think it is to have a panel, chaired by a judge?

9. What is the role of the independent member, the psychiatrist?

10. Does the composition of the panel make a difference to proceedings? If you had to lose one of the other two members, which one could you do without?

11. How confident do you feel about the decisions you reach?

12. What do you see as the main benefit of having a review?

13. Could you say whether you agree or disagree with the following:

    i.   One key role for DLP hearings is that no matter what the prospects for release, the prisoner's case gets seriously considered. [Prod: would you go so far as to say there is a therapeutic element to a DLP hearing?]

    ii.   Whatever else, DLP hearings contribute to the next stage of the life sentence process. They have a steering effect.

    Are you aware of the Parole Board Statement of Purpose? [The Parole Board for England and Wales exists to carry out risk assessments to inform decisions on the early release of prisoners with the ultimate aim of protecting the public. We aim to be fair, open and consistent in all our decisions and to operate effective and efficient processes in order to consider cases in a timely manner.]

14. How fair do you think the DLP process is?

15. How open do you think the DLP process is?

16. How consistent do you think the DLP process is?

17. How effective do you think the DLP process is?

18. How efficient do you think the DLP process is? [compare with other processes if helpful]

19. How formal/informal do you think the process is?

20. Do you think it should be more formal, or more informal?

21. One of the panel's main responsibilities is to look at risk. How do you assess risk, when preparing for and conducting a hearing?

22. How important are the following:
    - where the prisoner is in relation to the tariff
    - security classification
    - behaviour in prison
    - offending behaviour courses completed

- remorse
- release plans/home circumstances
- supervision arrangements
- the victim's view/circumstances
- any other key factors?

23. Do you tend to form a preliminary view based on the paperwork? How much time do you spend going through the file?

24. Your key role is in making decisions about release and transfer to open conditions. Given the nature of most of your hearings, do you feel your terms of reference are appropriate?

25. What is the role of the Secretary of State, the lifer governor?

26. How independent do you think the panel is in practice from the Home Secretary?

27. What sort of pressures are you under when making decisions? [Probe: Are there 'hidden pressures'?]

28. [If time – having said all that you have, can we return to the first few questions – if I were to ask you again...]

29. Is there anything else you would like to add?

Analytical guide for DLP observations[72]

Who is involved (including representation, witnesses)
Time
How agenda is set
Characteristics of prisoner
Sec State's view

Structure
Who leads the discussion?
In what order do proceedings take place?
Deviations from procedure
In what order do the penal members speak?
What issues are discussed; in what order?
How are issues addressed?
      are they addressed explicitly and in detail?
      do all members contribute to the discussion of topics?
In what ways does the judge control the hearing?
In what ways does the judge involve others?
Do the other panel members influence the order of proceedings?
How much planning took place for the hearing?

Establishing the evidence
In what ways is the questioning carried out (inquisitorial?)
Does the prisoner challenge any of the evidence?
Were any forms of evidence privileged?
Treatment of witnesses
Called by whom (and for what reason)
Is the reliability of witnesses explicitly questioned?
What type of information is sought?
What is the role of any witness called?

---

72. Adapted from Policy Studies Institute: Protocol.

Prisoner representation

Qualifications/relevant experience of legal rep

Length of time prisoners' rep

Does the legal representative challenge evidence/routes suggested?

What evidence does the representative bring up?

Is the representative acting under the explicit direction of the prisoner?

Does the prisoner suffer by not having a legal representative?

Impact on decision?

Decision reached

What was the process by which the decision was reached (examples of consensus/negotiation)?

Did any aspect of the discussion not appear in the recorded decision?

What level of agreement/disagreement was there?

Deliberation

Distinguish decision formulation from reasons for decision

Who leads the discussion?

What topics are discussed?

What time is devoted to the question of release, transfer, risk?

In what order do panel members speak?

Do all members contribute to the recording of the decision?

Are there issues not discussed?

Issues throughout

Legal/policy considerations

Nature of risk – including impact of courses

Insight/compliance – how was this linked to risk?

Release plans – at what stage discussed? what significance attached?

Contradictory evidence/disagreements

Discussion of recommendations

Factors which influence panel to make recommendations outside terms of reference

Appendix 4:   The role of the researchers and the research experience

Several aspects of this research project made it both enjoyable and satisfying. The team, and our deliberately different areas of expertise, made it a learning experience for each of us. It was at once daunting and profitable not to have all the information or expertise in one head. Legal and sociological dimensions of the decision-making process were pertinent. Teasing out some of the tensions between due process and other good practice considerations was one of the more testing research tasks we faced. We were fortunate to have on the team a full-time research assistant trained in psychology. The three disciplines we brought to the project: law, social science and psychology reflected, albeit imperfectly, the deliberately diverse structure of the panel.

The observations and our discussions of them taught us that our individual perceptions were different. This became more evident at the analysis and writing up stage. We saw the same events and heard the same dialogues; and we were all very detailed in our recording of what went on. Most of the time, we noted similar items and lots of verbatim speech. But our reading of the process was slightly different. The legally qualified member of the team perceived witnesses being called, and evidence being tested: a modified version of a court-like process. The social researcher perceived fewer of these formal processes: 'the judge turned to the prisoner and started to ask questions'; 'the independent member challenged the prisoner on his account of an offending behaviour course...' so that when we came to seek a consensus about the process we had observed and tried to describe it, we realised that we had to discuss 'what had gone on' in the room at considerable length. Our use of language was different (for example, the meaning of the word 'formal'), and our expectations were different. This was a creative process and we are satisfied that it has enhanced the quality of our account. Just like a panel, our biases and assumptions have been checked under the scrutiny of another member of the team.

There were, of course, painful and frustrating aspects to the research, as we became more knowledgeable about discretionary lifers and read detailed dossiers about their often very serious and complex crimes. We learned a lot about the difficulties of making progress in prison, the current limitations of sentence management for lifers and the forbidding task of assessing current risk in a severely constrained environment, often very many years after the offence. Prisoners sometimes had extremely high hopes of the DLP process; others had become so resigned they declined to attend. The average length of time already served by those whose panels we observed was 13 years and six months; the average tariff was eight years. All of the problems of long-term imprisonment were visible around the edges of our project, and were sometimes at the core.

One of the difficulties of method in this research was the lack of time available to build up relationships with establishments and panel members, although this did begin to happen where individual panel members appeared more than once throughout our short programme of observations. It was uncomfortable (especially at first) to be a visitor, often for only a day, and to launch straight into inquiry mode. The usual niceties and politenesses of 'entry into the field' were limited to a few pleasantries on the way in and out of each prison, as everyone, including ourselves, was there to do business. Despite this, we were treated with good grace throughout, except by a very few reluctant judges, who were unhappy about their deliberations being observed.

There were advantages to limited contact too. Despite the restricted nature of the contact we had with individuals involved in decision-making, one difficulty we all experienced in the project is related to this need to develop trust and dialogue with those involved in the process being researched, whilst remaining non-participatory, detached and firmly committed to our observer role. This is a delicate balance, and once the barriers are broken and trust established there is a natural tendency for those being researched to draw the researchers into the world of action and debate. It is tempting (and very occasionally, strategic) to join in. We resisted most of the invitations to share opinion (and sometimes inside information) with members of the panel during the informal stages of the process, seeking at all times to turn questions back to those who asked them, at which point they were usually happy to oblige. During the formal process, and the deliberations, we were strictly silent, and averted our eyes on the two or three occasions when individual panel members appeared to glance in our direction. It was not easy to be regarded at all times as 'a fly on the wall'. Some rooms made this more difficult to achieve than others, with room size and layout varying considerably between establishments. Panel secretaries (and occasionally judges) suggested where we should sit, sometimes with other observers. We usually had a good view of the proceedings, and preferred to be at a little distance from the panel's table. Once proceedings began, all the participants involved seemed fully engaged in the process, and we are satisfied that our presence made no impact on decisions[73]. The

---

73. If there was any impact, which we will never know, it could only have been to move proceedings slightly towards a more careful adherence to formal and due process procedures. This has certainly occurred in other criminal justice research (for example, in policy evaluations, where agencies can tend at first to seek a favourable outcome in the research. Researcher effects are also assumed sometimes, but not proven, in observational studies of police cells and adjudications), but we would be surprised in the light of what we have learned if the carefulness we observed during the DLP process was in any way the result of a research presence. We could check the decisions made at hearings we witnessed against a control group, but this would only give us a superficial answer to the elusive researcher effect question.

research process may have influenced panel members to reflect on their own (and others') approach to the task, and this, we assume, was not unwelcome.

In the end we were surprised by the level of co-operation we generated, sometimes to the point of awkwardness, for example, when we were treated following a hearing almost as sounding boards. Once a decision was made (and importantly, drafted) we felt a little more free to give as well as to take, but still, we hope, to a properly limited extent.

References

Agar, Michael (1980/1996) *The Professional Stranger: An Informal Introduction to Ethnography,* London: Academic Press.

Barnard, Elizabeth E (1976) Parole Decision-making in Britain, *International Journal of Criminology and Penology* 4: 145-159.

Bottomley, A Keith (1990) 'Parole in Transition: A Comparative Study of Origins, Developments and Prospects for the 1990s', in M Tonry and Norris, *Crime and Justice,* Chicago: University of Chicago Press pp. 319-374.

Bottomley, A Keith (1984) Questioning Parole: Whose Discretion? What Principles? *Prison Service Journal* 56 (October), pp. 21-24.

Bottomley, A Keith (1973) Parole Decisions in a Long-Term Closed Prison, *British Journal of Criminology* 13: 26-40.

Bottoms, A E and Brownsword, R (1983) 'Dangerousness and Rights', in J Hinton (ed), *Dangerousness: Problems of Assessment and Prediction* London: Allen & Unwin.

Burgess, E W (1928) Factors making for success or failure on parole, *Journal of Criminal Law and Criminology* 19(2): 239-306.

Clarke, D, Fisher, M and McDougall, C (1993) A New Methodology for Assessing the Level of Risk in Incarcerated Offenders, *British Journal of Criminology* 33(3): 436-448.

Coker, J B and Martin, J P (1985) *Licensed to Live* Oxford: Basil Blackwell.

Cullen, E and Newell, T (1999) *Murderers and Life Imprisonment* Winchester: Waterside Press.

Cross, R and Tapper, C (1999) *Cross and Tapper on Evidence* (9th Edition) London: Butterworths.

Dworkin, R (1977) *Taking Rights Seriously* London: Duckworth.

Gelsthorpe, L, Howes, M and Grounds, A (2000) *Clinicians' Decision-Making Regarding Medium Secure Units.* Report to the Department of Health, unpublished.

Hawkins, K (1983) 'Thinking About Legal Decision-Making', in J Shapland (ed) *Decision-Making in the Legal System.* Issues in Criminological and Legal Psychology No. 5 British Psychological Society.

Holloway, K (2000) *Mental Health Review Tribunals:The Release of Restricted Patients.* Unpublished PhD Thesis.

Home Office (2000) *Prison Statistics England and Wales 1999* London: The Stationery Office Ltd.

Home Office (1999a) *Report of the Parole Board 1998-99* London: The Stationery Office Ltd.

Home Office (1999b) *Lifers: A Joint Thematic Review by Her Majesty's Inspectorates of Prison and Probation* London: Home Office.

Hood, R and Shute, S (1995) *Paroling with New Criteria: evaluating the impact and effects of changes in the parole system: Phase Two,* Oxford Centre for Criminological Research.

Hood, R and Shute, S, with the assistance of Wilcox, A (2000) *The parole system at work: a study of risk based decision-making* (Home Office Research Study No. 202) London: Home Office.

Hood, R and Shute, S (2000) Parole *Decision-Making: Weighing the risk to the public.* (Home Office Research Findings No. 114) London: Home Office

Kitsuse, J and Cicourel, A (1963) A Note on the Uses of Official Statistics, *Social Problems* 11: 131-139.

Liebling, A (1992) *Suicides in Prison* London: Routledge.

McConville, M, Saunders, A and Leng, R (1991) *The case for the prosecution* London: Routledge.

Nash, M (1999) *Police, Probation and Protecting the Public* London: Blackstone.

Page, J (1998) *The Conduct of Discretionary Lifer Panels; discussion paper* (unpublished HO paper, LRU).

Parole Board (1973) Report of the Parole Board for 1972. HC 274, London: HMSO.

Sparks, R (1997) 'Recent social theory and the study of crime and punishment', in M Maguire, R Morgan, R Reiner (eds.) *The Oxford Handbook of Criminology* (second edition) Oxford: Clarendon Press.

Terry, Karen J (1999) *Analysing The Effects Of Motivation On Sex Offenders in a Cognitive-Behavioural Treatment Programme,* Unpublished PhD Thesis, University Of Cambridge.

Tidmarsh, David (1999) 'Necessary but not Sufficient: The Personal View of a Psychiatric Member of the Parole Board', in Murray Cox (ed.) *Remorse and Reparation* London: Jessica Kingsley.

Tyler, T R (1990) *Why people obey the law* New Haven: Yale University Press.

Walker, N (1996) *Dangerous People* London: Blackstone Press.

Weber, L and Gelsthorpe, L (2000) *Deciding to Detain: how discretion to detain asylum seekers is exercised at ports of entry* Cambridge: University of Cambridge, Institute of Criminology

Wood, D (1988) *Dangerous Offenders and the Morality of Protective Sentences* Criminal Law Review 424.

Woolf, L J (1991) *Prison Disturbances April 1990: Report of an inquiry* London: HMSO.

RDS Publications

Requests for Publications

Copies of our publications and a list of those currently available may be obtained from:

Home Office
Research, Development and Statistics Directorate
Communications Development Unit
Room 201, Home Office
50 Queen Anne's Gate
London SW1H 9AT
Telephone: 020 7273 2084 (answerphone outside of office hours)
Facsimile: 020 7222 0211
E-mail: publications.rds@homeoffice.gsi.gov.uk

alternatively

why not visit the RDS website at
             Internet: http://www.homeoffice.gov.uk/rds/index.html

where many of our publications are available to be read on screen or downloaded for printing.